CHINA, MY GREAT TEACHER

CHINA, MY GREAT TEACHER

Lu Shan, My Shangri La

HOW YOU AND CHINA CAN LEARN AND PROFIT

FROM THE MISTAKES OF THE UNITED STATES

Sid Anderson

Copyright © 2005 by Sid Anderson.

Library of Congress Number: 2004098923
ISBN: Hardcover   1-4134-7102-1
             Softcover   1-4134-7103-X

All rights reserved. No part of this book may be reproduced or transmitted in any form or by any means, electronic or mechanical, including photocopying, recording, or by any information storage and retrieval system, without permission in writing from the copyright owner.

This book was printed in the United States of America.

To order additional copies of this book, contact:
Xlibris Corporation
1-888-795-4274
www.Xlibris.com
Orders@Xlibris.com
24497

CONTENTS

CHINA, MY GREAT TEACHER
Lu Shan, My Shangri-La

The Thousand Steps 17
War, and Children 21
We were "Millionaires" 25
Population Explosion 27
Disease 29
Trends and Incidents 32
The Best School in the World 33
Hong Kong, the "World of Suzie Wong" 41
Returning to Japanese-occupied Shanghai 42
Birth & Death in 1st Grade 51
Tribute to Miss Bull 53
World War II 55
The Girl With the Red Rose 63
Farewell to China 66
We Visit China in 1999 67

HOW YOU, AND CHINA, CAN LEARN AND PROFIT FROM THE MISTAKES OF THE UNITED STATES

Sunrise, Sunset 75
1 : Breaking the Scales 77
2 : Where There's Smoke 82
3 : Bigger Sticks & Stones 85
4 : Incompetent Parenting 89
5 : Growing Debts, No Savings 92

6 :	$$ Billions For Pills	94
7 :	Wealth & Poverty	97
8 :	Buying & Selling People	99
9 :	Dreams of Winning	102
10 :	Gas Guzzlers	103
11 :	I Can't Go Home	104
12 :	Chemicals In My Body	106
13 :	"Call Now!"	107
14 :	My Father Can't Read	108
15 :	Gone With the Passenger Pigeons	109
16 :	Hopalong Cassidy	112
17 :	Chernobyl Couldn't Happen Here	114
18 :	Civilize 'em With a Cragg	118
19 :	Exponential Growth	120
Sunset, Sunrise		125

This book is dedicated to

Chinese students studying or proficient in English

(about 65,000 in the U.S. at any one time)
(uncounted millions in China)

wishing you

Health, Wealth, and Happiness

"It's been said that there are more English learners in China than there are native English speakers in the whole world."

Quoted by permission from Jeremy:

@1-language.com, Chinese Center,
where you can find free, quality materials
for learning English online, through Chinese

Since the numbers of people are so large, it is probable that no one could prove or disprove the above startling statement, but it gives us pause for thought.

The future happiness of the whole world
depends very much on how China and the United States
maintain friendly cooperation.

You and I

may be among the most important people in the world

because we can help this happen.

This book is in two parts:

The first,

CHINA, MY GREAT TEACHER
Lu Shan, My Shangri-La

is about my past, the true story of my own exciting experiences growing up in China, in the 1930's.

The second part,

HOW YOU AND CHINA CAN LEARN AND PROFIT
FROM THE MISTAKES OF THE UNITED STATES

is about our future. It can become your own true success story, if you choose. It can bring you Health, Wealth, and Happiness.

I was born on Lu Shan in 1922 and lived in China for the first 16 years of my life (except for two trips to the U.S.) My parents had arrived in China in 1915 as Southern Methodist missionaries, wishing to promote education, health, and happier ways of life. My mother taught English at a girl's middle school in Suzhou. My father worked in the country near Sungkiang. After five years they were married, moving to Shanghai where my father supervised building of the Moore Memorial Church (now MuEn Church) in the center of Shanghai beside what was then the "Race Course," now the People's Square.

I have always been happy that when my father first arrived in China, as was the custom, he was given a Chinese name which sounded similar to his name in English—"An" (Peace), sounding like "Anderson. The Chinese character for "peace" is the combination of "roof" with "woman" under it. One woman under a roof is peace, but, of course, more than one woman under a roof—can be trouble!

Much later, when I was at the Shanghai American School, a Chinese college student friend made me very happy by giving me Chinese characters for my first name "Sidney"—"Sih" for "snow", and "Ney" for "patience", together meaning "patience to bear the snow". (see my "chop" at the beginning of this book.)

You may wonder why my parents were "Southern" Methodists. During the Civil War (1861-65) in the United States, which was fought partly to end slavery, Methodists split into northern and southern branches. Years later they joined again to become the United Methodist Church. In the second half of this book I'll talk more about slavery and prejudice, among the most serious "mistakes" of the United States.

SID ANDERSON

In 1922 when I was born (I am a great grandfather), Lu Shan was a summer resort mainly for missionaries and international business people. Sadly, few Chinese were able to enjoy it in those years. Here is my story:

CHINA, MY GREAT TEACHER

Lu Shan, My Shangri-La

A shorter version—"The Last Days of KAS, My Shangri-La" was self-published in 1988 by my special friend Paul Sherertz in LUSHAN MEMORIES

This book is also dedicated

with love

to

the girl with the red rose

THE THOUSAND STEPS

Through freezing drizzle, scraping chunky ice from my eyebrows, I sweated to keep up with the coolie carrying my suitcase as we trudged (under huge ice-covered oiled-paper umbrellas) up the stone "Thousand Steps" of Lu Shan (Kuling), sacred mountain of central China. Startlingly like so many traditional Chinese paintings, waterfalls dropped from crags above the clouds into valleys revealed only momentarily through churning mist.

Marveling at the half-inch-ice covering my suitcase, I felt a surge of boyish pride for my new Voitlander camera inside, bought with $40 saved by going home 3rd-class on a Japanese river steamer to Shanghai—instead of 1st-class with the teacher-escorted group on a Butterfield & Swire British steamship (jacket-and-tie for dinner). I felt it was a neat trade. I had escaped first-class "baloney" for independence, and a new camera! I was 14.

I was born August 29, 1922 on this mountain at Dr. Barrie's Hospital (which still exists, I understand, as the Kuling Hotel or Guest House). I had spent several wonderful summers here, and now was returning to Kuling American School, KAS, after Christmas vacation, 1936-37, not knowing that less than a year later I would be descending these steps with my schoolmates, for the last time.

Shangri-La, in James Hilton's 1933 adventure novel, LOST HORIZON, was fantasy—a remote Asian mountain valley where unusual idealistic people lived wondrously healthy lives dedicated to preserving the best that civilization had produced, hoping it would survive a worldwide war. I was enthralled by the book, then by the 1937 movie, admiring Ronald Colman as my hero—but smitten with deep love for Jane Wyatt, singing Brahms' Lullaby with the village children, skinny-dipping in a waterfall pool!

It seems almost fantasy that (4000 feet above the rice paddies, 400 miles up the Yangtzee River) KAS actually existed, yet I remember it as yesterday—unusual idealistic people living a wondrously healthy life in a real high valley, dedicated to sharing the best of Earth's civilizations—and, sometimes, skinny-dipping in waterfall pools. It did not survive World War II as a school, but it did survive in the memories and lives of those fortunate enough to have been there.

During sixteen growing-up-years, China was my Great Teacher, Lu Shan was my own Shangri-La! What were the many life-changing insights I learned, from China?

as published in BOYS & GIRLS, 1964
1st printed in COLUMBIAN, 1940, Shanghai American School annual

We could never estimate how many people, unknown or famous, have written poems about LuShan. One of them was the young Mao Tsetung. He climbed Lu Shan on July 1, 1919 and wrote this poem in classical Chinese verse:

ASCENT OF LUSHAN

Perching as after flight, the mountain towers over the Yangtze;
I have overleapt four hundred twists to its green crest.
Cold-eyed I survey the world beyond the seas;
A hot wind spatters rain drops on the sky-brooded waters.
Clouds cluster over the nine streams, the yellow crane floating,
And billows roll on the eastern coast, white foam flying.
Who knows whither Prefect Tao Yuan-ming is gone
Now that he can till fields in the Land of Peach Blossoms?

from MAO TSETUNG POEMS,
Foreign Language Press, Peking, 1976

WAR, AND CHILDREN

As children, we naturally did more playing than thinking, but certain things were absorbed, from what we saw, smelled, heard, tasted, and felt all around us. We had seen or heard of abandoned babies from the slums of Shanghai—dead in the ditch—and also some who were rescued and educated, becoming leaders in the new China. I had smelled sailors sick-drunk in the alleyways.

I had seen three U.S. Marines in rickshaws, arrogantly shouting at their coolies to race each other, forcing them to run "like Roman chariots", not knowing (or caring) that coolies worked so hard and ate so little that they seldom lived to age thirty.

A Marine Lieutenant was our Scoutmaster for a short time in Shanghai, but knew nothing better to teach us than military marching, week after week. Finally we took it into our own hands and with the help of the church committee were lucky to find a new wonderful scoutmaster, Eugene Hubener—(thank you for everything you shared with us!).

We had tasted feasts, delicious beyond the outer world's imagining, yet seen hunger daily, so starkly real we could feel it. Though we ourselves had never been hungry, we knew hunger was agony—making health, education, happiness impossible.

We had been embarrassed to see tourists demanding service, acting so crudely, learning so little, that we felt ashamed they also were from the United States.

But, on the day that we left KAS for the last time, and started down the Thousand Steps, my feelings at the moment were excitement in the high adventure of setting off for Hong Kong. Under my lumber jacket (sent by Mississippi grandmother, but with holes chewed by pet chipmunk), under my sweater, old plaid shirt, and winter underwear, was a secret moneybelt with vast amounts of folding money (on deposit by parents for balance of school year) and on my back, a homemade pack. On that day in Dec. 1937 I was only dimly aware that the self confidence of a very shy boy had been given a tremendous boost by the high valley.

More immediately, war was very much with us. No bombs had fallen at Kuling, though Japanese planes had flown over in formation. We had several air raid alarms, spending hours in a sandbagged basement shelter. But now, only a few days before (on Dec. 12th 1937), Japanese planes had sunk the U.S. river gunboat USS PANAY, just sixty miles away, the immediate reason that our school was suddenly closing. We were headed inland, up-river by steamship, (away from the advancing Japanese armies), then south by train to Hong Kong, and finally up the coast by ship to Shanghai in Japanese-occupied central China—where the larger Shanghai American School, SAS, continued in the French Concession—and my parents worked at Moore Memorial Church in the International Settlement. The Japanese military had left these central parts of the city untouched for their own future benefit.

Our vivid experiences with war, however, had started years before. In 1932 I had lain awake long nights to the rumble of bombs, and shells from offshore battleships, like a continuing earthquake. The entire factory district of Shanghai had burned, the sky red from horizon to horizon. Ashes fell in our yard for days. On my way to school I could see the Japanese dive bombers, and felt "Hollywood excitement", but, after school, often saw endless lines of refugees surging into the International Settlement, carrying babies and a few remaining belongings. Children's eyes showed terror through their tears.

One day a Chinese bomber, in trouble, jettisoned a giant bomb, accidentally hitting a rush hour street corner only a few blocks from my father's church office. Over a thousand people were killed instantly, including my girl friend's father, Dr. Rawlinson. Even today when some movies seem to make war a "game" or "comedy", I can seldom laugh, for China taught me that war is real. For millions of children war is devastating, with lifelong agonizing consequences.

On this trip, as on a thousand occasions before, we were aware of being "different", American kids in China, often stared at by the village children and sometimes called "yang-kwei-tze" (Shanghai dialect for "foreign devil"). They had been taught by parents and grandparents who remembered soldiers from the U.S. and Europe marching into China.

Later I came to know Chinese students who were very much aware that nearly all the steamships, railroads, factories, and mines in China were owned by foreign countries. Slowly China taught me that, like it or not, we were a part of colonialism.

The famous Whangpu Park (on the Bund in Shanghai beside Soochow Creek), tradition says, had a sign on the gate: "No Dogs or Chinese Allowed". Long before the Japanese invasion, much of China had been "stolen" from the Chinese. The International Settlement and the French Concession in Shanghai were owned and operated by and for the Europeans. Even though it is mentioned as fact in a great many books, there are those who feel the above mentioned sign is a "legend", as no actual historical photos have been found. There is however evidence that there were probably two signs, one saying "No dogs allowed", the other saying "No Chinese but nannies" (caring for European children). The underlying intent, of course, is obvious. Even the website of a modern Shanghai hotel repeats this legend. A Chinese friend who grew up in Nanjing tells me that she was brought up to believe it was a fact that there was a sign in Chinese on the park gate saying: "Chinese and Dogs Cannot Enter". For those who would like to read a great deal more evidence, Google: Shanghai, No Dogs or Chinese Allowed.

Opium had not originated in China, though many people still think it did. In fact, it was virtually unknown, banned by the imperial government. It was grown purposely by the British in India to start the addiction in China, because early trading ships had nothing the Chinese wanted! The British had nothing to exchange for the silk, tea, and countless treasures which could make a ship owner's fortune in a single voyage. So, European gunboats blasted their way into the major Chinese ports with cannons (the "Opium War" 1840-42) forcing China to grant 99-year leases. No wonder we were sometimes called "Yang-kwei-tze", foreign devils!

WE WERE "MILLIONAIRES"

As kids we were actually very privileged. Even though my father's annual salary was only about US $2000, everything in China was so inexpensive that we lived "like millionaires." We had a nice home with two servants, a two or three month vacation every summer at the beach or mountains, even the beautiful mountain lake in Japan, Nojiri. When I was sometimes worried about this as a teenager, my parents explained that they came to China to teach, not to cook and clean house. Also, our servants and their families would have opportunities otherwise impossible.

However, I was very impressed by one young couple who came to China as teachers. They had no servants, dressed in Chinese clothes, and lived in a Chinese style house.

There were times when I felt an unresolved longing. Like Kipling's Kim, I daydreamed of dying my skin, and escaping into China, at last free to be myself, to pursue my life's adventures "unbranded". China taught me that sometimes it hurts to be considered "different".

Later, in Shanghai, some of us joined an association of international schools and, when asked to provide some entertainment from the U.S. at their show, we naively put on a "Minstrel Show", blacking our faces with burned corks and singing songs from the old south. We knew little of the history of slavery and prejudice—to be discussed in the second half of this book as one of our most terrible mistakes.

Lu Shan rises so abruptly from the Yangtze valley (with the vertical cliffs of "Lion's Leap" and spectacular "Three Falls" dropping over a thousand feet) that it has a climate all its own, very different from the steaming valley. Known in English as "Kuling", ("cooling") it had become a European summer resort, and then the summer capital of the Chinese government. Generalissimo Chiang had recently come to our school for an orchestra concert, together with body guards. My friend Paul Sherertz took a picture, but sadly, in his excitement he forgot to wind the film, and double-exposed a window across the Generalissimo's face!

I admired Madame Chiang, for, though her husband was trained as a military "war-lord", and possibly was still that at heart, she had been educated from early girlhood in the U.S. and graduated from Wellesley College as a thoughtful idealist, working hard to encourage the best for China, helping to start the "New Life Movement". As a college student I read THE SOONG SISTERS by Emily Hahn (Doubleday, Doran, N.Y., 1941), and was deeply impressed by their key roles in the history of China. As a teenager I possibly overly idealized her. There are those who tell questionable stories of some less idealistic chapters in her life, such as her association with Wendell Wilkie, U.S. presidential candidate. In the past quarter century she was abandoned by Taiwan and nearly forgotten by the rest of the world, living her final years as an artist recluse, dying recently on October 23rd, 2003 at age 105.

One morning before breakfast I was walking on a tree-shaded path above our school when I met them, walking alone towards me. I shyly said, "Generalissimo . . . Madame Chiang." They smiled.

I read Edgar Snow's, RED STAR OVER CHINA, the amazing story of the "long march," early days of Communism in China, and their many idealistic goals. But China taught me that it may not be enough to have valuable goals if the methods used to try to achieve them sometimes cause tragedy.

POPULATION EXPLOSION

Descending the mountain, we seemed to look straight down on fields and villages, to the far horizon. From our travels we knew a little of the great size of China, from the Great Wall to the jungles of Burma, from the ocean to the high plateaus of Tibet, backed by the highest mountains in the world, headwaters of all the great rivers of Asia. So densely populated is central China that every square foot had been reshaped by man. You can't find an inch of land which isn't a field, path, home, temple, or grave.

Reaching the foothill village, taking a bus to the Yangtze port of Kiukiang, we were suddenly again in the midst of the "teeming masses" of China. I remember two years later standing in line for hours at Nanking (Nanjing) railroad station, people packed so tightly we could only shuffle an inch at a time. One early morning I had squeezed my way past thousands of factory girls coming into Shanghai to work, some on "wheelbarrow-buses" (4-on-a-side, back-to-back), bicycles, trams, canal boats, and uncounted thousands on foot. My $40-saving river steamer had six triple wooden bunks to each cabin (no mattresses)—and maybe 400 more deck passengers.

Coming from Japan one summer, I had been amazed to see the ocean suddenly turn from blue to brown (a clear-cut line) far out of sight of land—it was the "Yellow Sea", the outflow of the Yangtze River (ranking with the Nile and Amazon as world's largest). For me it symbolized China's size, at that time 400 million, now over 1.280 billion. No wonder there were not enough schools. Even though education had long been respected and desired, it was only a lucky family who could pick ONE of their children to go to school. So, China taught me that world population is exploding—children everywhere beyond counting, many apparently with no one to love them. Even small problems obviously become desperate when children are hungry, sometimes even sold. Every child should be wanted, and loved.

As we made our way along cobblestone streets to the dock, familiar smells of China surged around us, the "Chinese national air." Padded winter garments were difficult to wash. Human excrement as well as animal manure was saved to return to the fields as fertilizer (an important secret of survival over the centuries). As kids we had a special name for the giant pottery vats on every farm. We called them: "honeypots."

DISEASE

Illness was always in sight, hospitals few. In October we students had spent a day vaccinating villagers for smallpox, each team of two having a Chinese student interpreter with poster explaining the benefits, and assuring the farmers they would not have to lose a day's work. We practiced on each other, sterilizing an arm with alcohol, spreading two drops from thin glass tubes of vaccine, then gently scratching the skin with up-and-down motion of a sterile needle held parallel to the skin.

After a long day, we were shocked on arriving at a dirt-floored farmhouse to learn that, right at that moment, a woman was dying of smallpox. I had seen thousands of pock-mark-scarred faces of lucky survivors, but remember mostly this one horrible glimpse of a still-living face. A few years earlier, we were told, there were thousands dying in these villages. China taught me that even when widespread illness seems overwhelming, progress can be made. 40 years later, news reported that smallpox was finally gone from the United States and many other countries, and becoming rare in Asia and Africa. Possibly our greatest challenge now is to make progress in preventing emotional illness.

As we boarded the Butterfield & Swire steamer and started upstream, with a British gunboat in company, we had a last look at Lu Shan, its shrub-covered but treeless peaks shrouded in snow and clouds. Yes, all central China, for 500 or more miles in every direction—was treeless—except for isolated giant trees in temple gardens. Lu Shan had one temple famous for its "Three Trees". Shrubs were harvested by "charcoal-burners", who roasted the branches in underground pits. They often brought baby animals to school to sell. We tried to raise a Muntjac deer's fawn, which tap-danced around our dormitory for days on 12-inch legs—till it suddenly died—saddening us all, more than we would admit. It had eaten excelsior (wood shavings) we had carefully put in its specially-designed "nest", not knowing any better.

We raised a wild boar, until it grew so big it gleefully raced around the school grounds, clipping us off our feet from behind like a football blocking-forward—so, with sadness, we were advised to let it go. There were chipmunks, hedgehogs, and others. But when two mountain lion cubs arrived in a basket, our headmaster wisely said we should not buy them. I was sad, yet China taught me that probably wild animals should never be made into "pets". Years later when I saw Scarlet Macaws rolling in mated pairs above the rain forest, I at last sensed the meaning of true "freedom", and could never again put a wild creature in a cage.

We kids had been shocked to learn that over the centuries as the population grew, trees all across China had gradually been cut as fuel, till there were no more. Then came floods and dust storms, growing deserts, and famine. We had seen pictures of the Yangtze floods taken from their plane by Lindbergh and his young wife, Anne Morrow, who thrilled us with her true-adventure book "North To The Orient". Their float plane was once endangered by desperate flood refugees trying to climb aboard. China taught me that a vast continent can be so reshaped by humans that, natural protections gone, it becomes open to catastrophe. Forests and grass, which over centuries had built rich topsoil (holding the moisture and preventing fast run-off}—were gone. The "Good Earth", millions of years in forming, was washing away into the sea.

As the throbbing engines carried us steadily westward against the current, Jim Harnsberger (my roommate) and I climbed to the top deck, then forward to the very prow, where a uniformed Chinese deckhand was sounding with a lead-line (just like on Mark Twain's Mississippi). Even 500 miles from its mouth the Yangtze was still nearly a quarter of a mile wide, but with constantly-shifting shallow mud-and-sand bars where we could easily run aground—as we actually did, briefly, later that day.

Fascinating junks of all sizes and shapes tacked upstream or surged down river, some having come through the famous and dangerous Yangtze Gorges, with whirlpools beneath thousand-foot cliffs. Now China is building the world's largest dam. Its future is yet unknown. What will China teach us about building giant dams?

TRENDS AND INCIDENTS

At Hankow we visited the U.S. Consul, who gave me a new official copy of my birth certificate, complete with red ribbons and sealing wax. Then we boarded an "international train" with huge flags of many nations on the roofs. The tracks to Canton had been bombed repeatedly in recent weeks. Would we become an "incident", starting a new phase of the war? Should missionaries or business people who make the personal choice to go to a far land (and get caught in some local conflict) expect rescue by their country's armed forces? It's a challenging question still agonizingly difficult to answer today.

We had already begun to realize that there are trends as well as incidents. In recent years I had spent long weekends helping to mail letters to U.S. Congressmen, asking that no more U.S. scrap iron be sold to Japan. It was well known that hundreds of freighters were steaming from California to Japan carrying our scrap to build Japanese battleships and bombs.

This trend became an incident three years later when U.S. scrap iron fell on Pearl Harbor.

I hope my missionary-kid moralistic upbringing isn't suggesting any easy "right" or "wrong". With good reason, missionaries worked at the long slow processes of education and health, trends in the right direction. And so, China taught me that in life, rather than being overly concerned about incidents, or trying to pinpoint the "blame", it may be better to work toward long range goals.

THE BEST SCHOOL IN THE WORLD

It was only when we were jolting away the endless miles south along the tracks, passing sandbagged stations where work crews were repairing recent bomb damage, the countryside growing greener and warmer (Mistletoe appearing in the trees), that we began to feel the sadness of leaving KAS. It had been a truly remarkable school. Everyone participated in everything. It was taken for granted. No one was left out, even though shy and on the fringes. Instead of overly competitive sports (where the best become heroes, and the inexperienced are ignored) everyone participated in daily "rec"—soccer, cross-country running, track-and-field, hiking, two four-day all-school camping trips, sledding, and scouts—it was in scouting that we learned the most.

On mornings of fresh powder snow, when we woke to a mountain winter wonderland, we carried our sleds a mile to the "Gap" at the head of Central Valley, for a fabulous non-stop run back to school—our eyes half-blinded by snow, streaming with happy tears—just in time for breakfast!

But the heart of our physical education program was a plan which made self-improvement the challenging goal. At the start of each term we were each tested for 100-yard-dash, baseball distance-throw, high jump, broad jump, etc. We improved during daily sports, but were also encouraged to practice these skills. I remember my deep satisfaction in discovering the next term that I had improved—a lot! I learned that training works. I was still in the lower third of the group, and knew it, but never felt belittled or looked down on. When I reached the U.S. I was amazed and proud to discover that suddenly I was in the middle third, and still improving.

KAS, with only about 65 students and 14 teachers, had two weekly mimeographed newspapers, and occasionally a third written by the grade school kids. Almost everyone was a reporter. I think, at one time or another, everyone was. We had much practice in trying to write simply, telling the "who, where, what, why, and how" of an event—cause and result. Hopefully we would learn to write in a way that would interest our fellow students and families— help them feel like "they were there." As a very shy kid I learned with surprise that possibly I could write better than I could talk, and gained minor fame in reporting the slaughter of a hog for Thanksgiving dinner: "Poor Pig!", which phrase ended almost every sentence.

We had some mediocre teachers, but also several who poured their hearts out to help us grow "in wisdom and in strength." Learning facts was secondary to learning processes, and practicing skills. Most important of all was a quiet effort (often consciously planned) to give each and every one of us responsibilities just within our capabilities, which could boost our self-confidence through "experiences of success." Then would come another tougher job to challenge us more, and bring further pride of achievement. It was not left to chance for a few outstanding students to grab all the proud moments. I can't think of anyone in the school who didn't grow through small successes.

China taught me that a child who grows up under repeated experiences of failure and defeat cannot break out of that sad trap. But, once one has had a few experiences of success, an occasional defeat can be taken in stride, and learned from. (As a parent I have pondered this very much, but it is far easier to preach than to practice!) But China taught me that in any teaching-learning situation the most exciting challenge is to help each and every child have experiences of success. (This concept became clearer to me much later, through the wisdom of, A.S. Neill, and his Summerhill School.)

In spring, Lu Shan was alive with flowering Azaleas, and a veritably noble custom existed at KAS on May 1st—"May Day". If someone should throw a flower at you, it was your immediate duty to run after them, and kiss them! And so, with each passing hour the shyness and inhibitions of overly-protective missionary-upbringing melted away amid laughing and running, the ground well sprinkled with blossoms. China taught me: "What is life without kisses?"

Thinking back, it's a shock to realize how few things of lasting importance took place in the classrooms. China taught me that people learn only from emotionally-charged first-hand experience. It's only after we have had a wealth of first hand experiences, that we can begin to learn from the words and experiences of others.

Kuling American School is loved as "the best school in the world", (without exception, so far as I know) by all who were there—but WHY?

1) The SETTING was magnificent!

Secluded, dramatically beautiful—a sacred mountain—rising through mists like traditional Chinese paintings. Sparkling streams, crystal pools above and below each waterfall, precipitous rocky cliffs, endless vistas, sunsets . . . Mountain Lions, wild boar, Muntjac deer, even "tigers" (or spotted leopards), still roamed the ravines we hiked.

The previous year, 1936, a KAS teacher, Mr. Lauridsen (at the request of villagers whose farm animals were being killed) had shot a spotted leopard "tiger". He did not hunt it for sport. (photo below, courtesy of his son, Peter)

In winter we had LuShan all virtually to ourselves.
It was my Shangri-La!

Legend says that poet Li Po (Li Bai) and companion, in their mature years, rode white horses up LuShan, disappearing into the mists—never to be seen again. But, possibly, we kids may have glimpsed them, through misty snow flakes . . . certainly we learned more than we were ever aware of—and are still learning—from the wisdom and experience of China, our "great teacher".

by Moon dehua, LuShan

SID ANDERSON

In LUSHAN MEMORIES, one of my schoolmates, Irene Vongehr Vinvent, in her HISTORY OF THE KULING AMERICAN SCHOOL, writes:

"From The Song of Lushan, Li Po, A.D. 701-762:

The Lushan looms near the constellation of the south Dipper,
   Like a nine-fold screen adorned with embroidery of clouds . . .
      The craggy ranges over-reach the azure blue,
         And girdled in pink mist and green foliage,
           They glisten in the sun . . .
              Lushan is my joy and inspiration.

More than a thousand years before the great Tang poet, Li Po, wrote so rapturously about Lushan, the mountain had held China spellbound. It is said that Lao Tse, founder of Taoism, wandered there with a friend, both riding white ponies. They were searching for the Tao, that is, the truth. When they found the Tao, they became immortal and vanished, leaving behind the hut where they had lived. So, the legend continues, the mountain was called Lushan, or Hut Mountain."

Legends sometimes build on legends. In my reading about Lao Tze, I find the story that, discouraged by people's lack of dedication in searching for the Tao, he finally traveled to the furthest western borders of China . . . and disappeared . . . riding on a water buffalo (or an oxen, others say.) Even the dates of his birth and death are mysteries. Some even suggest he made his way to India and was actually the founder of Buddhism!

There is a painting of Li Po, riding a white horse, with a riderless black horse beside him. www.poetrybootcamp.com He was known to be wild and rebellious, a lover of wine. One story says he drowned, trying to scoop up the moon's reflection in the river. Others say he died in Dangtu in modern day Anhui, probably of mercury poisoning from imbibing Taoist longevity elixirs. http://en.wikipedia.org/wiki/Li_Tai-Po.

Maybe better researchers than I can trace these legends to their source—maybe not. But the purpose of legends, I guess, is to inspire us—no problem there.

One thing is for sure: Each of us can ride our own white horses, searching for the Truth, seeking to build a better world, as we create our own "legends".

You will note in the painting, there is one riderless horse—could it be for you?

2) We were especially fortunate to have had unusual PARENTS, world-travelers, idealists, lovers of music and reading. We already had broad experience, and required little discipline, thanks to our families.
3) Our TEACHERS, many of whom had traveled half way around the world for this opportunity, were personally dedicated to helping each of us achieve our fullest potential, far beyond the classroom. In fact, those mostly-forgotten classroom hours were a very minor part of KAS. A boarding school is a 24-hour learning experience.
4) Our three school papers, already mentioned (ECHO, Junior Echo, and Echolette), helped us learn to share our special experiences.
5) EVERYONE WAS INCLUDED in every activity. It was just assumed, not left to chance or choice, that everyone would participate in everything. No one was left out because of shyness, or even a speech defect.
6) We had SCOUT TROOPS, far more important than classes, probably unmatched in the world (opinion, yes, but show me better ones!) We spent long hours, by choice, studying up on merit badges. And, never to be forgotten, we had fall and spring camping trips—to Pig Valley, Po Yang Lake sand dunes, and other exotic places.

Many will remember, as vividly as I do, the last night at KAS, when "Keller" (Jean Paul Keller, Scoutmaster) woke us at midnight in the boy's dormitory for a farewell party. He told us we were "the greatest bunch of kids in the world". I would say, the luckiest—no, it wasn't "luck". Thanks to careful planning and dedicated concern by parents and teachers, we were—the "most fortunate."

7) And, of course, Mrs. Allgood, who made the school our "home"—fresh-baked bread, hot cinnamon toast in mid-morning, and wonderful food! My parents say that in my first letter I wrote: "The food here is wonderful. We always get all we want, and sometimes all we can eat."

Any school, of course, is the sum-total of all who were there that particular year. KAS, for me was 1936-37. The last year, weeks, and days. Thank you, KAS!

HONG KONG, THE "WORLD OF SUZIE WONG"

Finally we reached Kowloon, on the mainland side of Hong Kong harbor. It was Jan. 1st, New Year's Day, 1938! The weather was like central Florida. Still with homemade backpacks and sweaty winter clothing worn night and day since leaving, we walked into the elite Peninsula Hotel—very British! They had converted a lounge into a dormitory for us, packed with thirty or so cots.

Three friends and I (Jim and Hutch Harnsberger, and Don Whitener) having no adult supervision and finding that it would be two weeks before we could catch the next overcrowded ship to Shanghai—discovered a much cheaper room down the street. We moved out—to spend two carefree weeks exploring Hong Kong on our own!

We rode bicycles to the far reaches of the city, spent chilly days on deserted beaches at Repulse Bay, voyaged on the harbor ferries endlessly night-and day, took the cablecar to the Peak, explored exotic markets and boat villages, snacked on dumplings at steamingly-aromatic street-restaurants, window-shopped—spending hardly any money! Once, deciding to splurge, we took a sampan out to the famous Floating Restaurant, dining like kings!

Without Hollywood's glamorization, we saw the real "World of Suzie Wong". Of course, as missionary kids, we were not tempted by street girls, though we were very aware of their brazen presence, and they sometimes approached us. We saw beggars, fancy weddings, funerals, street children. In those two weeks of intense personal experience China taught us a great deal about the joys and agonies of real life on the streets, alleyways, and waters—of Hong Kong. Today, as an 81-year-old grandfather, it still seems—like yesterday.

RETURNING TO JAPANESE-OCCUPIED SHANGHAI

The Italian "S.S. Conte Biancamano", by far the largest ship I had ever been on (torpedoed a few years later), was so overcrowded with refugees returning to Shanghai that meals were served in shifts far into the night. Not brought up in an olive-oil-bath, I survived on bread, cafe-ou-lait (how do you say that in Italian?), and an orange each breakfast.

Shanghai harbor was as crowded and busy as ever, but looked "different". From every single available pole or rooftop flew "fried eggs", our name for Japanese flags. Destroyers and cruisers were moored right in the center of town, with torpedo-sabotage-resistant nets around them.

I had day dreams of blowing one up, using all sorts of sneaky submarines and disguised sampans. However, my missionary background had exposed me strongly to non-violent methods for achieving goals. Not wanting to kill any mother's son, but still wishing to blow vast military installations to "Kingdom Come", my imagination finally found its ultimate plan in occupied Nanking during a vacation in 1939.

On our way to an ancient tapestry-weaving guild we passed an airport—endless rows of Japanese fighters and bombers, lined up as far as we could see—only a single barbed wire fence between us. I would commandeer a fire truck, fill it with gasoline, drive along the road at 3 AM spraying gasoline from the firehose, drenching every line of parked planes—light a match at the far end, and flee! Because unfulfilled, that fantasy often recurs.

How naive! Even if no Japanese soldier were killed, I would have been caught, creating an international incident. Far worse, Japanese retaliation would have been swift and merciless, a second rape of Nanking. Hundreds of thousands died in the first.

But, amazingly, the tapestry guild was far more memorable. From a busy street we entered a high-walled doorway into a very old rambling tile-roofed building with many wings. It seemed dark inside, fairly quiet but with a rhythmic clicking from many looms, giving a fascinating effect of syncopation. There was a pleasant fragrance of silk fabric and possibly incense (from an unseen family alter in the back?).

The looms were tremendous, four-to-six feet wide and possibly over twenty feet long. They made us feel small as we watched with whispered exclamations of amazement. There were two operators at each loom, one handling dozens of different colors of silk thread bobbins, and about twenty foot pedals.—the other, high up under the ceiling, pulling a maze of levers and strings to control the pattern. "The more we gazed, the more our wonder grew." Patterns were unbelievably complex: landscapes, birds, beasts, temples, people in multi-colored robes—not repeating for several feet or yards.

The handsomest of all, in blue and gold, held us quietly watching for a long time. The elder, our guide, told us calmly that it went to a monastery in Tibet, which had a standing order for a certain amount each year . . . "forever." We left in stunned silence. In the midst of an enemy-occupied city these craftsmen were continuing quietly in the traditions of their ancestors. Our teachers had told us how, time after time through history, China had "absorbed" its conquerors. I knew this was an exaggeration, for millions had suffered and died in the process. But, China taught me that though emperors and generals may come and go, customs and patterns of daily life, passed on from family to family, change very slowly.

Being a "Nature-Worshipper" at heart from an early age, I had been impressed by Peking's Altar of Heaven—three levels of white marble, a perfect circle. Like the ancient emperors, I too had knelt at the center of the top level—nothing visible but the sky, in all directions. I admired the person of long ago who had designed it for the emperors. China taught me that to gaze in wonder at the starry heavens, is much more emotionally moving and life changing than to "worship" an idol.

In China we were constantly reminded that we were in an old culture. It was impressive as a teenager to visit temples, intricately decorated in lacquer and gold, which were already a thousand years old when Columbus sailed (he thought) to the "orient". I had touched, and heard the spine-tingling reverberating boom of the largest and oldest bell in the world in Peking, weighing 50 tons, making the Liberty Bell seem a mere trinket. I watched a craftsman carving a chest, intricate figures covering the entire surface. He had been working on that single piece—for seven years. To a twelve-year-old that seemed an eternity.

I remember the emotional impact of climbing along the Great Wall, near the point where it reaches the sea, about 20-feet high and equally thick—continuing out of sight up and down steep mountains for (though it seems incredible) over a thousand miles! I have learned since that there were many sections, built at different times, most crumbling, some rebuilt.

We sometimes talk of the "wonders of the world"—the pyramids, Roman buildings, temples of Central America—as if they were a wonderful benefit to the world. Then someone mentions slave labor. We slowly realize that all of these masterpieces, designed by some genius in the employ of the ruler, yes,—but hardly possible without slavery. It is estimated that possibly two million died building the many sections of the Great Wall. In crumbling remains it is said that bones of thousands have been found inside the Wall itself.

Incredible manual labor was in sight daily. Rickshaw men seldom lived to be thirty. Huge cargo barges were towed by hundreds of men, tethered like draft animals. In the Yangtze Gorges they had been known to be dragged into the whirlpools to drown. I had watched ships being loaded by endless lines of coolies, sweat bands and breeches dripping, bones visible under their skin. I never knew how many hours they worked, how many coppers they received, or how many others depended on their work, but their faces told the story—hunger is agony. China taught me that when humans are little more than beasts of burden, "slave labor" is only a matter of degree, and it is fitting to secretly cry when we marvel at the "wonders of the world."

Shanghai had over five million people (today over fourteen million) and was one of the world's comparatively "open cities", where people came from all over the world. Thousands of "white Russians" found new homes there during the Revolution. We sometimes bought bread at "Countess Olga's Bakery" on Ave. Joffre.

One afternoon after school I went to the 1939 Hollywood movie, "Balalaika", about the Russian Revolution. Deeply moved, walking out of the theater into the evening sunset, I realized that those around me, mostly women, were weeping. They had relived their own personal experiences.

Recently, seeing "Dr. Zhivago" again, it was all brought back to me as Tanya tearfully recalled her earliest memory (I realized that she too might have ended up in Shanghai): "My father and I were running through the city and it was on fire. The Revolution had come and we were trying to escape—he let go of my hand—he let go of my hand!—and I was lost." The Comrad General said: "Tanya, Komarov was not your real father. Zhivago was your real father and I can promise you, Tanya, that if this man had been there, your real father, he would never have let go of your hand."

Then, in the tearfully happy ending, Tanya, balalaika over her shoulder, walks away with her powerdam operator boyfriend. The Comrade General asks him if she can play—"beautifully! She is an artist!" I wanted to buy a balalaika, but never did. Maybe I still will—for Tanya.

The most agonizing memories—of Tanya—have deeply affected my life—street children, some abandoned, some sold. Even in our "best" families, how much of the world's sorrow has started with some adult—letting go of the hand of a child?

Then came Hitler. Truly remarkable is the story of the idealistic Chinese consul-general in Vienna, Dr. Ho Feng Shan (1901-97).

With a PhD in political science, fluent in German and English, he had a wide circle of friends including many Jews, very active in the intellectual and social life of Vienna. Single handedly he made it possible for several thousand Jews, fleeing Hitler's holocaust, to obtain free visas to Shanghai. (Google for details) (Read his exciting story in Shanghai Star, Apr. 11, 2000).

These refugees arrived with little money but many skills from their rich heritage. Some carried a few family treasures, such as linens, which they were forced to sell to survive. Shanghai already had a symphony orchestra. Suddenly there were two—but many skilled musicians found it difficult to find jobs.

My mother met one, Mr. Rose, and signed up my best friend, Bill March, and I for singing lessons. A musician who should have trained the best voices in China had to settle for two kids, rank beginners! I remember the stories he told us before and after lessons: of skiing in the Vienna Woods—he urged us to learn if we had the chance. I did, and always remember him when I ski some fresh powder trail in the early morning. He also told us of a fascinating doctor named Sigmund Freud, and his own deep disappointment in missing the opportunity to go deeper into his work. He urged us to learn more about Freud. I did, and it opened pathways to developmental psychology, Reich and Neill. Thank you, Mr. Rose . . . and Dr. Ho.

My mother was a liberal, widely read and interested in the views of everyone. She met a young Chinese college student who secretly was interested in Communism (life-threatening in Shanghai in those years), but she invited him to our home for long conversations.

As a high school student in 1939 I was becoming more aware of colonialism and its often cruel grip on China. I admired Chinese college students when they were frequently outspoken. As a sometimes rebellious teenager myself I once accused my father of being prejudiced against the attitudes of these students. He responded that this was not true at all, that he had been deeply concerned and usually supportive of student opinions through the years, had even testified on their behalf in a terrible shooting which he witnessed not far from his church office in Shanghai.

One day recently, in late Oct. 2003, I got a phone call from my cousin Dan Sullivan, recently retired from the U.S. State Department, telling me with excitement that during part time routine survey of old State Department files he had accidentally come upon the records of this "Shanghai Incident", including my Dad's testimony. He mailed me copies of about 50 pages, taken from File 893.857: Report of the International Commission of Judges appointed to inquire into the causes of the "disturbances" at Shanghai, May 30th, 1925. (I have added the quotation marks). No Chinese were invited to take part in the Commission.

In the proceedings the following excerpts from "background information" were included: (b) "Chinese residents of the city of Shanghai have no part nor representation in the government of the city. (c) In all cases, whether civil or criminal, where a foreigner is a party by or against a Chinaman, a foreigner is in fact the judge. (f) projection of roads into Chinese territory without authority of the Chinese Government; (g) Extension of the Government of Shanghai into Chinese territory over said roads;"

The following were listed among the "Immediate and Proximate Causes: (a) The killing of Chinese laborers by Japanese in cotton mills; (b) That said Japanese were not criminally prosecuted; (d) strikes in various cotton mills occurring almost daily; (e) open and notorious agitation by members of Labor Unions; (f) agitation by persons of bolshevistic tendencies; (k) full-page articles by thirty-one Chinese associations for weeks before May 30th;(m) The failure to release students who had been arrested prior to the 20th day of May; (t) failure to suppress gambling and abuses generally, including illicit traffic in opium;"

My father witnessed this shooting of students on Nanking Rd. in front of the police station from within 40 paces. His testimony covers 12 pages. He felt that the group of approximately 200 students were approaching the police station to support their friends just arrested. A large crowd of passersby had gathered, stopping traffic, but the students were not violent, had no sticks or arms, were only shouting slogans with some banners, walking slowly. "About 3 or 4 foreign police and an equal number of Chinese and Sikhs were pushing the crowd back. I saw one (student) with blood streaming down his face."

As the first shot rang out my dad, right in the line of fire, jumped into the doorway of an electrical shop. Then there were 50 to 100 shots from the line of about 20 police across the front of the police station. "I saw some 10 or 12 boys and men lying in pools of blood at various places on the street. I would say absolutely unjustified." He saw no intention of "capturing" the police station, no cries of "Down with the foreigner or "Kill the foreigner", none whatever. When asked if he was biased against the police, my father replied: "I am not whatever. I may say, to prove it, that the Nanking Rd. Station, Louze Police Station, has been of very great service to the institution for which I work."

Dr. Cline was also a witness, saying he had been handed a pamphlet in an orderly manor by students on Nanking Rd.

In contrast, was the testimony by a Mr. Maitland: "I am going to prove that the students . . . a better word would be schoolboys . . . ignorant and conceited . . . came from a Bolshevik University—the Shanghai University of Seymour Rd. . . . pure Bolshevism and nothing else . . . the police in these riots acted with the greatest leniency and the greatest reluctance to fire, and the only reason for the firing was because it was impossible for any human being to do otherwise and keep order in the Settlement. There are certain lies being circulated in the Settlement that people were shot in the back. I am calling medical evidence to prove exactly where everybody was shot."

Other witnesses report: "When the main crowd was within twenty or thirty yards of the entrance, Inspector Everson stated that he gave the order to present and the armed party was in full view of the advancing crowd. He also said that before giving the order to fire he ran five yards towards the advancing crowd waving his pistol and shouting in English 'Stop, or I will shoot', and in Chinese, 'Stop, or I will kill'.

Finding that the crowd did not stop, the inspector ran back to the armed police and gave the order to fire which, owing to the din of the crowd (or reluctance of the officers?—author's comment), appears not to have been heard.

The Inspector then seized the rifle of the Sikh standing next to him, and fired at the crowd; and then the rest of the police, who consisted of eleven Sikhs and eleven Chinese, fired a somewhat ragged volley, but he said the result was more like independent firing . . . he gave the order to fire again. The second volley stopped the crowd and effectually dispersed it."

In his summary and concluding remarks, E. Finley Johnson, Chairman of Commission, made some interesting remarks, including: "Third. Nearly four hours before the regrettable part of the disturbances occurred, the Police Department had been notified that it 'must take special precautions' little or nothing was done until it was too late to prevent what happened. Fourteenth. That the foreigners in China have failed to take into account the principles of liberty and independence which they themselves have, by precept and example, spread abroad throughout China, concerning which the young rising generation have been apt students. Fifteenth. That the Chinese people have begun to take on a new civilization . . . have made greater advancement during the past ten years than in any one hundred years during their entire history . . . that they have begun to insist upon an honest and efficient administration . . . if they are to survive as an independent nation, they must have a larger and more direct participation in the affairs of their government."

Each year, on May 30th, I will go to a quiet place, and give silent tribute to the students of China on that tragic day, and through the years. I know many of you will join me.

In the late 1930's Shanghai was possibly the most international city in the world. There were communities of several thousands from each major nation. Track meets were like mini "Olympics". Chinese students often beat us in sprints, but we won at 880 and mile. I was told it was basically because we had better food—a sobering thought.

The Shanghai American School, with a huge campus of maybe 15 acres in the heart of the French Concession residential area, had a boy's dorm, girl's dorm, dining hall, water tower, gym, track, and playing fields—and far at the north end past the girl's hockey field was the bike house, and the small first grade schoolhouse. It was a far cry from KAS, but was an excellent school. Most of the approximately 500 students were children of U.S. missionary, business, and military families. A few were from international families who wished their children to go to college in the U.S. It was a "prep school", and a very good one. Except for my year and a half at KAS and half of 6th grade in the U.S. I had been there since first grade right through to graduation in 1940. I had vivid memories of that little first grade schoolhouse.

BIRTH & DEATH IN 1ST GRADE

My dad took me, that first day, past the huge gravemound, to the schoolhouse door—and left me. I can't remember the teacher's face or name, but can "see" BIG flash-cards . . . DOG . . . GIRL . . . we were learning to read. Classroom dim memories have faded, but outside, during recess and play, we experienced exciting real-life adventure.

I'm sure parents and teachers were unaware, but we discovered that the gravemound was crumbling, caved-in bricks at each end. A first grader could squeeze through, into the dark interior! The giant mound (6 feet high, 10 feet long, covered with grass) still seemed solid. Our teacher knew we climbed it, but, that we crawled inside—was our dark secret. Crawling, I dimly saw a brick-walled 3-foot high vault, dry, dusty, no odor—but—there was a bone, and a skull! Ribs, huge leg bones, silence, bits of light at the far end challenging me to go through rather than turn back. Others had been inside before me but my overpowering emotions, rather than fear of the dead, were of being a "first explorer"—as I emerged into daylight under the bushes near the gate to the street.

Tragically, that street corner was to bring a far more agonizing experience of death. A girl, just our own age, was killed by a truck, possibly while scrambling out from her rainy day rickshaw tarpaulins. I think she was actually a schoolmate. Infinitely beyond our understanding, this sudden close experience with the mystery of death brought terrifying sadness.

But then came Spring! Excited first discoverers of new bright outdoor mysteries, we ran, shouted, soared in swings, reveling in the joy of wind and sun on our faces.

Beside our schoolhouse was a thatch roofed open sided dirt floored shed—it was our gym. Hearing birds nesting in the thatch, we climbed the bamboo rafters, high up, until close to the nest openings. As a bird flew out past my face I peered into the darkness and could dimly see her eggs. Reaching in, I held one in my palm—it was warm! I was amazed, since it was still quite chilly. But soon there were baby birds, beaks wide open, announcing their hunger from dozens of nests, a noisy joyful Spring! (Rachel Carson, author of SILENT SPRING, must have been a teenager. It was 1928.) We were beginning to believe that soon we would be 2nd graders in the BIG SAS main building!

A few year later, learning that the world was round, some friends and I decided to tunnel straight down "to the U.S."—but we hit water at 3 feet. No wonder gravemounds were necessary in the Yangtze delta. But now, with the technology of modern China, a subway runs past our old SAS campus. I can't remember 2nd, 3rd, or 4th grades, except dimly—the first excitement of writing my own short story with pencil on lined paper—but 5th grade suddenly seems like yesterday, especially my science teacher.

TRIBUTE TO MISS BULL

Miss Grace Bull, I can see her now, carefully putting the thinnest membranes of a living frog's foot under the microscope, so that we could actually see the blood corpuscles circulating through the capillaries! Her love of Nature was shared with us in so many ingenious ways. As my turn came to look, she told me quietly that the same self-regulating life process was going on in me, in every finger and toe, night and day!

Another week, making aquariums and terrariums, she helped us catch the excitement that, possibly, they could be "balanced". Covered, they would create their own water cycle and would not have to be watered—yes, we could see the drops of condensation dripping from the glass cover, like rain from the clouds. With algae-eating fish, others to clean the glass, and small predatory fish which could survive on the tiny animal protozoa reproducing in the water—maybe, ideally, we would never have to feed them! Plants would give off oxygen, taking in carbon dioxide—while the animals took in oxygen and gave off carbon dioxide—like a miniature Blue-Green Planet Earth!

I tried it at home, with small successes, and some major catastrophes. I put in too many fish—over population killed them all. I washed the tank with household cleaners, and even though I rinsed it, again all my new fish died—of chemical pollution. Over the years those quiet exciting days in Miss Bull's class helped me gradually learn that I was part of Nature, not just a resident.

My excitement grew when on vacation I went with best friend Bill March to his father's Hangchow College biology lab where I saw a series of carefully preserved embryos of many mammals—dogs, cats, pigs, humans—amazed to see their similarity. I could hardly tell them apart. We humans even had tails before we were born! Experiences and insights gradually grew over the years. I too became a science teacher. Thank you, Miss Bull!

WORLD WAR II

I went with a German schoolmate to the German School to see news reels and Hitler Youth films, which met with openly mixed feelings from the audience. None were fooled by seeing Hitler with a baby in his arms. World War II had begun. China taught me that we are all, without question, citizens of Earth, whether we choose to be or not. Whatever we are involved in we should try to see in world-wide perspective.

It became an afternoon hobby (unknown to parents or teachers), to ride our bikes to the edge of the French Concession, through an often unguarded barbed wire barricade and out into the untouched battlefields. The trenches and bomb craters were half filled with stagnant water, sometimes a hand or head protruding. I even bounced a rock off a sunken head, ashamed inwardly of my crudeness but feeling a real need to make sure that what I saw was real. We collected helmets, bayonets, even grenades. One day, on returning, we met a group of loud arrogant Japanese soldiers. We three were lined up and slapped in the face by a young officer. Our trips ended when a schoolmate, Bill Hanson, lost several fingers when a grenade he had found—exploded. My own favorite collection, given me by Dr. Daniels in Nanking (after a tour of the hospital, including watching an operation), was a handful of shrapnel and bullets he had removed from wounded civilians.

One young teacher, Ted Herman, by telling many stories with obvious personal enthusiasm, was able to help us understand a bit of what was happening in the world. He was interested in the Chinese Industrial Cooperatives, which were small wartime village industries, scattered across the countryside rather than large city factories. Instead of all the profits going to a boss-owner, income was divided evenly among the worker-members, an exciting idea! Bob March, older brother of my best friend, managed a coop grocery store in Berkeley, California. When I visited, he invited me to their folkdance class. I was impressed that a store could be a community of friends, and came to love international folkdancing.

Another day Mr. Herman challenged us to try to look at the world from the point of view of a Japanese militarist—not so easy! When Japan was "reopened" in 1854 it soon became evident to them that the countries of Europe (in order to assure customers for hometown factories) had been busy carving up Africa and South America into colonies, and methodically "discovering" and claiming dominion over every island in the seven seas (not bothered by the fact that people had been living there for thousands of years.)

Japan saw that the United States had "explored" away a continent from the Indians, using bullets only when tribes, "unreasonably", were reluctant to leave their ancestral homelands. "Proudly", the U.S. had grabbed Puerto Rico and the Philippine Islands (as well as parts of North America) from Spain. When China was "developed" with the aid of European gunboats, the US invented a neat "gentlemanly" policy, demanding of China every privilege forcibly won by any other country, the "most favored-nation policy".

So, the Japanese militarists discovered that they were a few years "too late."

They tried valiantly to compete in normal trade, and soon managed to fill the stores of the world with cheap items "Made in Japan." The story goes that they even renamed one town "Usa", so they could print "Made in USA". Fair competition was a long slow process, too slow for the militarists. They decided to take over China, neighboring countries, and the islands of the Pacific, to make a giant new Japanese Empire. They would call it "The Greater East Asia Co-prosperity Sphere".

We did not change our feelings about the Japanese military, but our thoughts about the rest of the world (including the U.S.) did "grow" a bit. So, China taught me "history" and "economics" not usually mentioned in schools or books.

As an only kid, vacations in Hangchow with the March family, broadened my life. They had four boys and a girl, so I balanced things out with three on each side of the dining room table. For Saturday breakfast there would be a waffle iron at each end going full blast. On our bowls of oatmeal we had iced cold buffalo cream, better than ice cream!

Coming and going from Shanghai, when the train stopped at a station, we used to run up and hop in the engine. The engineer and fireman would only laugh. The engine bucked and jerked, making us wonder if it might jump the track. We were most impressed by the fireman. Shirtless, dripping with sweat, he would hose water onto the finely chopped coal, before shoveling it into the roaring firebox. Otherwise it would virtually explode and not give maximum heat. China taught me another lesson in the manual labor which kept colonial China roaring.

At that time a new bridge was under construction across the Hangchow river. Hollow concrete caisons were built beside the shore, floated out to their permanent position, then filled with concrete and sunk in place. We dove off of these and swam in mid river, hopefully checking the speed of the current first. Bill and Sher were better at everything than I, but looked out for me, so I was always challenged to improve.

One day when they were busy for an hour they loaned me their slug gun. I never thought of target practice and went out to shoot birds, soon killing one—to my amazement. I was shocked to be greeted with serious disapproval rather than praise. As part of my "lesson" I watched and helped the biology lab assistant clean, stuff, and mount the bird. I remember vividly how he carefully removed all the flesh, dusted skin and bones with chemicals to prevent rotting, refilled the space with padding, and wires to hold the stuffed bird in lifelike position. I never again shot a creature with a gun.

One day we rented bikes, taking them on a river boat to the next town up stream. At lunch we were in a second floor restaurant when a serious fight broke out on the street below. Both men were bleeding. In typical Chinese custom, a crowd gathered, each man turning to the crowd, presenting his side of the conflict to this "instant jury".

When it gradually became clear that the crowd was more and more supporting one man, the other slowly quieted down, finally walking away. Maybe we should learn from Chinese culture, and get rid of our entire legal profession! China taught me that most problems can be talked through to a solution.

After lunch it was cross country by bike back to Hangchow. On one steep down hill Bill and I were not careful enough, sideswiped each other ripping out many spokes—probably my fault. It was a long walk back to Hangchow, then to endure endless cursing from the bike shop owner. I only hope we had enough money to settle it fairly. Having an allowance that seemed small to us, we often forgot that we were "millionaires" in colonial China.

During my final high school year, 1940, Bill March, another friend, and I dreamed up a new after-school pastime. At the nearest street corner we would hop on the back of one of Shanghai's thousands of flatbed trucks. The coolies and driver would laugh, but never made us get off. We went to the ends of the city, then caught another truck back. If one turned the "wrong way", we just hopped off at the next corner and caught another one headed "our way". And so we spent many an afternoon discussing the problems of the world (such as girls), what we would do when the U.S. entered the war (for we knew it would), wondering what college days would bring, what we wanted to do with our lives, girls, religion—and always back to girls.

What did China teach us about sex?—sadly, not much—more questions than answers. I did learn that sex was a most powerful part of myself, and apparently everyone, on an international scale. I sensed, and fervently hoped, that love-with-sex could be the heart of life, in the future, but, sadly, at the moment we kids seemed "locked out". I wondered if confusions in sex and religion were inter-related, but that came in retrospect.

What did China teach me about religion? Maybe we had better forget that one! Close around us were just about every form of organized religion this round world had produced, each actively offering their "way". I saw the huge Catholic Cathedral School at Zi Ka Wei where thousands of children were rescued by their orphanage, to become life-long Catholics from a very early age, obviously a very "successful" program.

In many Sunday schools I was taught by "fundamentalist" missionaries who believed that the Bible was literally the word of God—stressing "salvation" from "original sin", thus avoiding "hell" and looking forward to "heaven". It all seemed a little too "simple". I personally was more and more challenged by the few who worked for a more "abundant life" now, stressing one's own conscience, motivated by love—obviously not simple. Watching any mother and baby made it clear that LOVE is the best way of life—but I obviously had some pretty nasty streaks within me. It wasn't easy, being loving—by choice—maybe impossible? Was this "original sin", or the result of growing up in the agonies of a somehow fouled-up civilization? Could a loving God allow millions to suffer through lifetimes of helpless misery?

Religions of China were also concerned with these problems. Buddhism which I saw around me, prayer wheels and fortune sticks, seemed more superstition than a way to happiness, but I only saw it from a distance. I did feel that China along with the rest of the world, did not have all the answers. What were the origins of mankind's foul-ups? Great and fascinating mysteries remained. So, China did not teach me all the answers

Finally came our SAS class of 1940 graduation, marching to the music of "Pomp & Circumstance"—farewells—one after another my friends left for the States. As kids we had led an unquestionably privileged life in China, sadly not sharing deeply in the lives of the Chinese people. Our schools did not even teach Chinese language, only a little history and culture. Some who lived in country towns learned more Chinese, but I forgot all mine at age four during a year in the U.S. when my mother was recuperating from tuberculosis in New Mexico. My parents said I refused to speak Chinese anymore when there were no more Chinese around me, even though they tried. But my dad returned to China, and my mother was an invalid. Back in Shanghai for first grade, I relearned only enough Shanghai dialect to barely "get-by". Maybe they should have brought my Chinese "ahmah" with us to New Mexico so that I could have continued to improve in Chinese. Then China could have taught me far more.

I was now old enough to take a deeper interest in the church community-center where my parents worked. I was often bored by services and sermons, but other activities impressed me. It was possibly the largest 7-day program of any city church in the world, some 2000 people coming there each day.

There were clubs for young men and women of all ages, who met socially to have serious discussions about their life problems in this huge changing city—fifth largest in the world. One was called the "Nine Naughty But Nice Girls—the 3N's." After getting to know each other they wanted to do something of real value, so started a school in a slum area. They changed many lives, including themselves.

There were three choirs for various ages. A shoe shine cooperative for homeless street boys did not intend to start them on a life of shining shoes, but gave them a start at independence, suggesting exciting goals they had never dreamed of.

Almost daily I heard a new story of almost unbelievable changes: from the slums to college, orphanage to medical school, or merely from tragedy to hope. Some haunted my memory—abandoned children, sometimes rescued from "baby towers", taken into orphan schools (one run by Brother Burke, close friend of my parents.) So, China taught me that ancestry and conditions of birth can be of minor importance in relation to opportunity, friends, and good experiences at the right time. A person becomes the sum-total of all they have experienced, but their own spark of freedom may be stifled early, causing them always to be victims of circumstance—or, may grow through experiences of success, allowing them to personally choose future opportunities! So China taught me that maybe "free will" is an "art" which can grow slowly—

but only for those fortunate to have experienced love, and success, in early childhood.

There were innumerable other lessons which China sneaked in along the way. Some "Christians" are capable of being mean, prejudiced, dishonest, even cruel—while some "heathen" seem naturally friendly, even loving. Possibly no one can begin to find happiness till the basic necessities of food, shelter, and health are met, but, satisfying these still does not guarantee happiness. Undoubtedly I "slept through" other important lessons.

Some of my Chinese friends stand out in my memory. "Shani" Yih was a college music major (spoke little English, but was eager to learn) who loved Strauss. He had seen the movie, "The Great Waltz", three times, choosing Johann's nick-name as his own. As I already told you, he gave me a Chinese name, with characters matching the sounds of "Sidney—Sih Ney", in Chinese meaning "patience to bear the snow". I was quite proud of the card he had printed for me in Chinese and English, and later had a traditional Chinese "chop" made to use with red ink (see cover of this book).

In contrast, George was an all-American boy in a Chinese skin. After spending most of his childhood in the States, he came back to China for a visit, but hung around with me for most of one summer, because he spoke little Chinese.

We had a few Chinese schoolmates at SAS, but they were just good friends. We never thought of them as different. When dancing with Elsie Lee at a school dance, I wanted very much to ask her for a date, but, sadly, never did—only because I was still a shy missionary kid, who had never yet had a date with anyone! Social life, till then, had always been in groups.

I did have a girl friend, a very important one, truly love at first sight. When I arrived back at SAS after leaving KAS via Hong Kong, the school was in the midst of putting on an athletic show in the gym. From a distance I saw a girl, in red shirt and white shorts, with a quiet serious expression, and quite beautiful. In the coming months and years we gradually got acquainted, went for walks around the campus. I took her to the formal athletic dance, for the first time wearing a tuxedo (borrowed from Dr. Cline who lived at our house). A short time later I went with her, and a group of friends, to the Grand Theater to see Gone With The Wind. I don't remember much of the movie, because I asked her if I could hold her hand—she said, "yes." We were both shy missionary kids. Even in the moonlight, when I took her back to her dormitory after the dance, we never kissed.

THE GIRL WITH THE RED ROSE

One day on the "Bund", the harbor main street of Shanghai, after seeing a friend off on the SS President Taft, I had an experience so moving, it seems like yesterday. A young Chinese girl, dressed simply, pants and jacket, all in black, came walking towards me—with a red rose in her hand. She came close, wanting to pin it on my shirt. Her eyes were soft, and bright.

I knew what she wanted. I had seen many brazen street girls, but this one was different, for she was just about my age, and lovely. I was emotionally moved.

She came so close I could sense the warmth of her body, see the moist glow in her eyes, feel her breath on my face—as she reached up, trying to pin the rose on my shirt. I was intimidated—but somehow stirred in a new way. I was being treated as an adult.

I refused her rose-invitation—and walked away—but inwardly gave her part of my heart. To this day I secretly realize that I wanted to offer her, not money, but hopefully some opportunity for a better life—and, let's be honest, I had fantasies of sharing love with her.

No, I didn't have any desire to go with her as a customer. My limited experience equated prostitutes with venereal disease. At a biological supply store, buying chemicals for my little home lab, I had seen a full color model of frightening sores from syphilis around the genitals, made I assumed for educational use in some medical school or biology class.

My fantasies in future months went far beyond the moment, to imagine what might have been.

What if she could have had the opportunities I was so fortunate to enjoy. She might have become a teacher, a doctor, or whatever she chose to be. Then we might have been friends, even lovers.

But, at the moment, what could I have done? In retrospect, I wish I had not walked away. My thoughts went back to the "Nine Naughty But Nice Girls" who had so impressed me. After meeting weekly for a year as a club for business girls, they were motivated to "do something worthwhile", so started a school for homeless children in the slums.

I could have pulled a sheet of SS President Taft stationery from my pocket (which I had just swiped from the steamship lounge) and written a note for her, something like this:

> To the 3N's, Nine Naughty but Nice Girls, Moore Memorial Church, 316 Yu Ya Ching Rd. This girl-of-the-streets needs help in finding a new life. You can probably open new opportunities for her far better than anyone else in the world. Thank you, A boy-of-the-streets, on the Bund

As I handed her the note I could have pointed west, down Nanging road, and told her in my fumbling Chinese how to get to the church. But could I have motivated her to actually go there? I knew that someone was expecting her to bring home money, maybe under life-threatening conditions. Like so many children of desperate poverty, maybe she had even been sold by her own parents. Should I give her some money, so that she would feel free to go to the church?

I might have walked there with her—it was only about a quarter of a mile—but I don't think I was up to that. I was shy. People would have looked at us, walking together, laughed, and made comments. If my Chinese had been better I might have been able to convince her that it would be very rewarding for her to go, but I wasn't up to that either. So—I walked away.

Over the years I've often thought of her, wondering and imagining what her life became—sad, I'm afraid, probably tragic—and what it could have been. With my encouragement, and help from the 3N's, the whole world could have opened for her . . .

We were both 16, our lives meeting for only one brief moment—like birds passing at sea . . .

*   *   *

FAREWELL TO CHINA

Towards the end of summer, when it seemed I had said goodbye to everyone I knew, my own sailing day came. I stood uncomfortably with my parents on the deck of the ship, seeing the tears close in my mother's eyes, sympathizing with my father as he, in fumbling words, wished me wonderful experiences in the United States.

I felt more expectation than sadness as the ship left the mouth of the Yangtze (not guessing that in 1980 we would have a Shanghai American School 40th anniversary class-of-'40 reunion in Washington, DC, and a 60th in 2000! Several wonderful KAS reunions were even better).

As the ship churned eastward, the Yellow Sea turned blue. I imagined the peaks of Lu Shan far beyond the glow of Shanghai lights, still brightening the western sky.

Unspoken thanks were forming within me, to grow steadily over the years—thanks to China, my Great Teacher—thanks to Lu Shan, my Shangri-La.

Many dramatic changes have come to China. Amazing what can happen in one short lifetime! New generations have been born, trying to learn from the past so that their lives can be happier.

Beneath-the-surface, under the veneer of politics, I wonder what we will learn from China—tomorrow?

WE VISIT CHINA IN 1999

In April, 1999 I took my wife, Ali, to China, my first time back in 59 years! Rather than going on an organized tour, I planned the trip myself so that Ali could see all the wonderful places where I grew up.

Leaving New York City, our jet took the northern great circle route, first pioneered by Lindbergh. His wife, Ann Morrow, was radio operator, and wrote the book, NORTH TO THE ORIENT, which thrilled me as a teenager, inspiring me later to become a private pilot.

If you take a piece of string and stretch it on a globe from New York to Shanghai, you will see that the shortest route does not pass over the ocean, but goes almost to the Arctic Circle. The Lindberghs made 17 stops for fuel (which had been sent ahead at great cost in money and labor, by plane, ship, and dog sled.) Our jet made only one stop, Tokyo, but we saw many of the same remarkable sights.

It was April, but soon after take off we saw snow below us, then an icy wilderness—no roads, no houses, many frozen lakes—it was the Arctic tundra, total wilderness for hours. Then, even more dramatic, we passed over the ice covered Rocky Mountains of Alaska, and the drifting ice flows and icebergs of the Bering Sea near the Aleutian Islands and Kamchatka, Siberia. Then we came down over the northern islands of Japan, made a quick change of planes in Tokyo, caught a glimpse of snow-capped Mt. Fuji, the Yellow Sea, finally Shanghai—after 17 hours.

Our trip came just three days after the unforgivable bombing of the Chinese Embassy in Belgrade, Yugoslavia by the U.S. It was claimed to be an error, targeting a white building, using an outdated map, when the real target was a supply building, also white. It was a tragic mistake by the U.S. Many advised us to cancel our trip, but we did not even consider that. We immediately told everyone we met in China that we were among many hundreds of thousands in the U.S. who do not believe war is a good way to solve problems, but are in favor of education and cultural exchange.

After a very few hours of sleep, our guide drove us south to the mouth of the Hangzho River to catch a fast catamaran boat to Putuoshan, where at age ten I had gone with my father when he planned a summer conference for 200 students. They used the off-season rooms at a Buddhist monastery, which is still there, somehow escaping the Cultural Revolution. We saw young monks at lunch, then running to the laundromat, were told they have a five-year "trial period", then can return to normal life if they choose.

Putuoshan, a Buddhist island, is very beautiful, a glimpse of old China, wonderful sea food, views of mountains and ocean, ancient temples. After a few short hours, we went by boat to Ningbo, jet to Nanchang, then by car with our guide, Vicki and driver, Liu, to Lu Shan where I was born and went to boarding school. Ali could feel my excitement!

We hiked in rain and mist, visited the buildings which had once been Kuling American School, were not able to find the hospital where I was born or my family's summer cottage, met a large group of elderly Chinese from Hong Kong, saw thousands of Azaleas in bloom. LuShan is now completely reforested, with mature trees over fifty years old, as we saw in many other parts of China, even along railroads.

(Note: In May, 2004, shortly before this book was sent to the publisher, my email friend in LuShan, Moon dehua, told me that after almost fifty years of no sightings a spotted leopard "tiger" had been seen that month on the rocks at ShiMenJian Valley (Stone Deer Valley) near Immortal Cave, an exciting extra reward from reforestation and environmental improvement!)

In Nanjing, with the help of our guide CiCi, we found the giant tapestry looms which had amazed me as a boy (now protected and still operated by the Brocade Institute, 240 Eastern Chating Rd.) Photos and samples of brocade for Tibet were on exhibit.

Then a marvelous visit to a kindergarten teacher training school, amazed that their course lasts five years, each teacher learning dance, piano, violin, singing, art, etc., far more than U.S. teachers are required to learn. We joined two classes of children at lunch and were especially impressed by their quiet friendly behavior.

We did not visit the Nanjing Massacre Museum. Dec. 13 is the anniversary. Each year air raid sirens sound to remember when the Japanese military entered Nanjing "allegedly with orders to wipe the city and its population off the map. Over several weeks, soldiers murdered an estimated 300,000 citizens by machine gun, bayonet, beheadings, rape, burning, drowning, and burying alive." During construction "hundreds of skeletons were exposed including beheaded babies, children, young and old piled on top of each other." There are books by John Rabe, Iris Chang; rebuttals by Tadao Takemoto, Yasuo Ohara.

In Suzhou we visited a middle school for girls which may have been the one where my mother taught, but early records had been lost during the Cultural Revolution.

In Shanghai we visited Mu En Church, on the way passing couples having ballroom dancing class on sidewalk, the wonderful new museum in People's Square (so fascinating we went back for second visit), the Children's Palace where their class was a concert for us, sidewalk view of the former Shanghai American School (now the Shanghai Marine Equipment Research Institute), then a few blocks north to my home in 1939-40 (amazed to meet four elderly Chinese neighbors who remembered my father after 59 years!). Among other experiences we were astounded by acrobats, TV tower, and 84-story skyscrapers. When I was a kid the tallest was 22 stories.

In Beijing I once again knelt at the center of the Altar of Heaven, as the Emperors had (only the sky visible). Tradition says they prayed for a good harvest. I gave silent tribute to the wonderful Universe of which we are a part.

Nearby, we talked with Canadian couples with their newly adopted Chinese girl babies.

At the Great Wall I asked our guide, Eddie, what we should do if we saw Mongol invaders coming on horseback, make smoke signals? or run! He said, "Don't worry. I have my cell phone."

At Beidaihe we visited beaches where I spent three wonderful summers, tried to find the hilltop cottage where I stayed and rode horses, but could not find them. Now there are mansions, hidden behind high stone walls. At the Under Sea World we walked through plastic tunnels surrounded by tropical fish and sharks. There were few visitors that day, so we had seven college student guides, and became friends!

On the train back to Beijing a young woman, sharing a seat and exchanging life stories, chose Ali as her "adopted grandmother."

Our China trip ended, far too soon, in Yangshuo, just south of Guilin. Exploring markets, eating at wonderful sidewalk restaurants, marveling at what is probably the most spectacular scenery in the world—a perfect place to end our China visit.

We went with Emily on bicycles far through the rice fields for lunch with her friend on a farm (see author photo on cover), a hike up to Moon Hill, finally a river trip where we were joined by a woman carrying two squealing piglets in baskets.

On our last night, we were "guest teachers" at the English Language School. Once again we wanted to tell them that the bombing of the Chinese embassy in Belgrade had happened just three days before we came to China, and that we are among many hundreds of thousands in the United States who do not believe war is a good way to try to solve problems. We believe in education and cultural exchange. In the dormitory we were given a farewell concert on Chinese fiddle by Chan Up, the young student who invited us, the last of so many new friends.

We were sad to leave China. Flying back over the arctic to the United States, we had time for many thoughts.

I wondered if the girl with the red rose might still be back there somewhere—a great grandmother in the new China?

I began thinking of writing the second half of this book.

* * *

Hello, again. This is the second part. The first was about my youth in China, a true story. The second is about our future, still an untold story. It can be a very exciting one, if we choose, filled with Health, Wealth, and Happiness! All I am going to do is tell about a large number of very sad—mistakes—we have made here in the United States, and suggest ways you can learn from them, and make your own future much happier.

Once again, I think we can agree that the most important thing in the world in this century is for China and the United States to follow paths of mutual benefit.

You and I are among the most important people in the world, because we can help this to happen.

We learn—from experience, so this book will concentrate on learning from the past—for a better future.

HOW YOU, AND CHINA, CAN LEARN AND PROFIT FROM THE MISTAKES OF THE UNITED STATES

SUNRISE, SUNSET

At sunset or sunrise, like me, you have probably sat on the beach looking out over the ocean—dreaming of the future.

But, unless we develop some powerful solutions not yet discovered, it is almost certain that in our grandchildren's lifetime all the world's present beaches will be gone. The streets of New York and Shanghai will be under the ocean—because of mistakes of the United States.

Sadly, we will talk of this more fully in Chapter 16, Gone With the Passenger Pigeons.

This sounds like a very pessimistic note on which to begin. I agree. But, as we learn and profit from the mistakes of the United States, we and our children and grandchildren can search for solutions—even have satisfying and happy lives—no matter what happens in the world. And maybe—you—will find solutions.

CHAPTER 1

Breaking the Scales

Here in the U.S. we have made so many mistakes it is hard to know where to begin, so I will start with the most visible, the first thing you can see on any street in America. You guessed it. Yes, in 2004 66% of Americans are—FAT—and getting fatter—up from 30% in 1983—up from 61% while I've been writing this book!

We were not born that way. It is not genetic, not in our genes. We became fat by making mistakes—mistakes in our diet, mistakes in our life style.

My father, like most Americans of his time, grew up on a small town farm. As a boy he plowed the corn field barefooted behind a mule. His family ate fresh home grown vegetables and very little meat (like country people in China). He worked hard, ran and played a lot outdoors, walked to school, learned to swim and play tennis. Other fresh foods which his family did not grow themselves, they bought at the local market.

Over the years in the U.S., food became big business, "manufactured" in factories, packaged in boxes, sold in super markets. To keep it from spoiling, chemicals were added. The parts which spoiled most easily (often the most nutritious parts, like the wheat germ) were removed. Salt, sugar, and other preservatives were added so that the product would have a "long shelf life." Then, because so much of the healthiest parts had been removed, the factory added a few vitamins—to make it sound good— "enriched". Americans now bought mass-produced patented products, "ready to eat"—instead of natural foods from the farm.

Animals are given hormones to make them grow bigger, crowded into huge feed-lots to fatten them quickly, injected with antibiotics to try to keep too many from getting sick. These hormones and antibiotics are still in the packaged meat, eggs, and milk bought at the super market, damaging the health of the innocent consumer.

Lazy Americans eat away from home more and more often at "fast food" restaurants which give "free" toys to their children, serve overly salted "French fried potatoes" loaded with fat, hamburgers dripping with cholesterol—which will soon form plaque in their arteries—leading to heart disease and death at a young age. At home they eat more and more packaged foods, "ready to eat" after quick heating in the microwave oven.

For some strange combination of reasons, parents, worried that their children won't eat enough, are constantly nagging them to eat everything on their plate—even though there is overwhelming research evidence that those who eat less—will live longer and healthier lives. And of course, if children have healthy food available, they will eat when they are hungry. Why make a big issue of it?

Each year the U.S. spends more and more on doctors and hospital bills (the "medical establishment")—yet the number who die from heart disease, diabetes, and cancer keeps growing. And the number who are grossly overweight keeps growing also. Something is seriously wrong. The U.S. is obviously making some very dangerous mistakes.

In the USA over 80% of deaths are from heart disease, diabetes and cancer, while only 12% of calories are from unrefined plant foods. Contrast this to Asian countries (Korea, Thailand, and Laos, or Chinese farm families) where only 5% die from these killer diseases and 92% of calories are from fresh vegetables and fruits. www.whi.int/whosis Food&AgrOrgofUN

Diabetes has increased 27% in 5 years, 17 million diagnosed, 12 million more developing the disease.—Center for Disease Control & Prevention.

Obesity is becoming so extreme that bariatric surgery, "stomach stapling", is up from 50,000 in 2001 to over 100,000 in 2003 alone! Newsweek, Dec. 8, 2003.

Is it in the genes? All agree that hair and eye color, shape of nose and number of toes—are genetic, but in recent years the U.S. trend has been to consider genes as the cause for almost all human traits, from intelligence to crime, from musical talent to depression and mental illness—downplaying the roles of experience, education, and environment. Could this be partly a subtle escape from responsibility? We may never know the complete answer, but some feel our future could be happier if we devote our energies to the aspects of our lives, and the lives of our children, over which we do have choice and control.

Researchers in health and medicine who stress genetics, are becoming more and more verbal. An example is a 1999 advertisement by Agilent Technologies stating: "Most disease is genetic. The faster scientists can sequence DNA, the faster they can pinpoint the causes of disease so cures can be developed." Some feel this is one of the major errors of our time. Genetic research will help us learn much about the history of mankind, but may not help us avoid cancer, diabetes, heart failure, or obesity.

Many are trying to do something about their health. They buy fresh vegetables at farmer's markets, "organic" vegetables grown without chemical fertilizers or pesticides. They shop at "health food stores". However, these health food stores have become such big business that even there many products are packaged, not as truly natural as they once were.

The government is recommending more vegetables, but 25% of vegetables eaten are fried potatoes.

Homeowners all have grills in the backyard to cook hot dogs, hamburgers, and steak—all dripping with fat. Then they buy the latest diet book, and try one plan after another. But, after losing a few pounds they usually gain it right back, plus a few pounds more. They drink "diet soda" with less sugar per can, but often fill a huge bag each week with empty soda cans—seldom drinking water—not knowing that soda is addictive, and not a good thirst quencher anyway. (two recent books tell the details: FAT LAND, How Americans Became the Fattest People in the World, by Greg Critser, 2003. FAST FOOD NATION, The Dark Side of the All-American Meal, by Eric Schlossen, 2002.)

If you listen to conversations anywhere around the U.S. you get the impression that we are working hard on the problem, but, sadly, with little success.

"In spite of the more than $110 million consumers spend—every day—on diets, and reducing programs (more than $40 billion per year), Americans are the most obese people in history. To be considered obese, more than one third of a person's body must be made up of fat. A whopping 34% of all Americans are obese, and the problem is getting worse, not better."—EAT TO LIVE, Dr. Joel Fuhrman, M.D. 2003, p.5.

This has been called our "weight loss industry". No one has counted how many people are profiting financially.

Autopsies show that even teenagers killed in car crashes already have plaque building up in their arteries, which will someday kill them. Our doctors die younger than the average citizen.

Pharmaceutical firms are most interested in patentable drugs for chronic ailments. One wonders if they have much interest in prevention, or cure. You might think that health care professionals would be happy when hospital rooms are empty—just the opposite—they want them full. It's all part of the $$ multi-billion medical establishment. At the YMCA where I exercise there are many comparatively healthy people who seldom see doctors, but we can't list our Y membership fee as an income tax deduction.

A news story about Okinawans in the March 30, 2004 N.Y. TIMES is a shocker. After long ranking number 1 in Japan in longevity, they have recently plummeted to number 26. Influenced by U.S. servicemen, and a rapid increase in fast food restaurants, slim Okinawans have become Japan's fattest prefecture. The first McDonalds opened in 1979. Okinawa now has more fast food than any other area of Japan. Even though they are the shortest, they now average the heaviest. They used to walk, but now drive big cars, have become sedentary. Many weight-loss centers are opening. We have not kept our mistakes to ourselves, but, like diseases, have been inflicting them on others around the world.

Okinawa is a dramatic story (like a controlled experiment) for on this small island there can be no doubt as to what caused the rapid change in life style, weight, and health.

CHAPTER 2

Where There's Smoke

The people in the USA who have made the second big mistake are not so easily recognized by sight, but you can smell them. Their clothes smell. Their homes smell. Their breath smells. Their fingers and teeth turn yellow. They have a very unhealthy dangerous life-threatening habit—SMOKING.

Tobacco companies spent billions and used every trick to get people addicted—using pictures of movie stars smoking, cowboys and other hero figures (like the "Marlboro Man"), to catch new addicts while they are young.

Here is "A brief history of smoking in America:

1492 Columbus "discovers" tobacco
1612 First tobacco plantation in America
1761 John Hill declares snuff to be cause of cancer of nose
1864 First cigarette factory opens in U.S.
1889 Langley, Dickenson landmark study of effect of nicotine on human nerves
1900 Four states ban the sale of cigarettes. Most other states follow, but all state bans are repealed by 1927
1930 Researchers in Germany find a statistical correlation between smoking and cancer
1950 Three major scientific studies link smoking to cancer
1964 First Surgeon General's report on Smoking and Health
1966 Health warnings on cigarette packages begin
1969 Congress passes Cigarette Act removing tobacco advertising from radio and television

1987 Congress bans smoking on airline flights of less than two hours
1994 Mississippi becomes first state to sue tobacco companies for costs of health care associated with smoking. Many other states soon follow.
1998 Attorney generals of 46 states sign an agreement with tobacco industry to settle state lawsuits.
1999 Philip Morris Co. admits that smoking causes cancer
2000 U.S. Supreme Court rules—against—the regulation of tobacco by the Food and Drug Administration!
Sources: Chemical Heritage Foundation www.tobaccofreeqc.com

We have made some slow progress. In 1965 42% of adults smoked
In 2001 23% still smoke
Source: Centers for Disease Control and Prevention

Yes (I admit it) I myself smoked for twenty years. I'll tell you how they caught me. One night in New York City I got free tickets and took my date to a radio quiz program called "Light Up A Camel". I was selected from the audience, won four cartons of Camel cigarettes—and started smoking—just what they wanted!

Twenty years later, as a science teacher, I took a course at New York Medical School in anatomy for non-medical students. Someone had assembled a display of lungs from autopsies, half from smokers (whose lungs were gray or black) and half from non-smokers—whose lungs were pink. I immediately started trying to stop smoking, but it was still hard. The Surgeon General began to publicize health studies, and warnings were printed on cigarette packages. Lung cancer and other diseases could be caused by smoking. Cigarette manufacturers were forced to pay millions in law suits. I finally stopped, forty years ago—and haven't smoked since.

Here are the annual causes of death in the United States:

Tobacco	430,700
Alcohol	110,640
Adverse reaction to Prescription Drugs	32,000

Suicide	30,622
Homicide	20,308
Licit & Illicit Drug-Induced	21,583
Anti-Inflamatory Drugs Such as Aspirin	7,600

"From 1990 through 1994, 2,153,700 deaths were attributed to smoking . . . the leading preventable cause of death in the United States."—US Centers for Disease Control

In recent years as more and more people stop smoking, the tobacco firms are now targeting young people in Central America and around the world, sound trucks giving away free cigarettes, huge Marlboro signs on shores of Lake Atitlan, Guatemala, one of the most beautiful places in the world.

It is amazing that they succeeded in tricking us into sucking deadly smoke into one of the most tender parts of our bodies! But you are smart, and can learn from our mistakes.

Even though we have made some progress, our problem with smoking is far from solved. The New York Times, March 10, 2004, reports that "tobacco is still the leading cause of death, killing 435,000 people" in one year. Centers for Disease Control and Prevention. Even in the small state of Connecticut where I live, cigarettes will kill an estimated 4800 people this year.

Tobacco firms are still promoting smoking in movies. "In Sony Pictures' Mona Lisa Smile, a recent PG-13 film, smoking is shown 21 times and there is a scene that prominently features an ad for Camel cigarettes!" Campaign for Tobacco-Free Kids.

CHAPTER 3

Bigger Sticks & Stones

The third mistake of the United States has left many hundreds of thousands dead, including women and children. It has warped the personalities of other thousands who were unable to lead normal lives when they returned home. This tragic mistake is—trying to solve problems by WAR—as in the Vietnam War, and many others. Many believe that the real problems can only be solved by education, cultural exchange, getting to know each other.

For instance, the "Cold War" between the United States and the Soviet Union went on for many years. Munitions manufacturers made huge profits. The whole world was put at risk of atomic war. Then, slowly, a few people traveled back and forth: sports teams, dancers, musicians, students. They made friends, went back home, told their families about their experiences. Some Americans began traveling to the Soviet Union to visit their relatives, and the villages their parents or grandparents had come from.

But we, the United States, did the unthinkable. We researched, built, and were the first and only nation to use atomic bombs. We destroyed an entire Japanese city of civilians—twice—Hiroshima on Aug. 6, 1945, Nagasaki three days later. We publicly condemn atomic weapons, yet we are the only nation ever to use them in war, even when many of our own generals and leading citizens were against it, feeling the war was already won. This happened before most of you were born, so I recommend you read HIROSHIMA, Pulitzer Prize-winner John Hersey's "most significant piece of journalism of modern times". See the motion picture, "Dr. Strangelove."

Among those who openly spoke out against using the atom bomb were General Dwight Eisenhower (later to become president), Admiral William D. Leahy, former President Herbert Hoover, General Douglas MacArthur, Albert Einstein, and many others. For details: Google-Hiroshima, Who Disagreed.

The husband of a friend of mine was a scientist at Los Alamos where research for the bomb was secretly done. Even some of the leading participants (probably including J. Robert Oppenheimer, Director), when they slowly became aware of what they were involved in, felt the bomb should never have been used on civilians. Another close friend married a Japanese survivor of Hiroshima who was among so many who later died of cancer. No one knows how many people around the world died from radiation, from the many worldwide atomic tests. We, all the world's peoples, are still suffering.

When so many were against using the bomb, why did we do it? As in all wars, there were many powerful people and businesses who would make $$ billions. By the end of the war, propaganda had so hardened us that few Americans could imagine Japanese families and children as human beings like ourselves. Only a handful had ever been to Japan. I was lucky. I spent the summer of 1936 at Lake Nojiri, climbed a volcano after a hot bath in a wonderful village spa, was taught folk dances by Japanese students.

But the decision makers in the U.S. were already "committed" to use the bomb. After all, we had spent millions to make it. We had little understanding of Japanese culture, unable to realize that if Japan were allowed to keep their Emperor, they would be willing to surrender. Maybe we should require our presidential candidates to have traveled around the world in their youth, maybe served in the Peace Corps (a U.S. Government project.)

That was not the end of our use of atomic bombs. We began years of "testing"—in the atmosphere, not knowing—or even seeming to care—about probable longterm effects on our children and grandchildren, around the world. At Bikini Atoll we used a Hydrogen Bomb. "The mushroom cloud was 8 miles across and

27 miles high. The canopy was 100 miles wide." The Hydrogen Bomb Homepage

In all we "tested" at least 1030 atom bombs between 1945 and 1992. At Enewetak, in the South Pacific, an entire atoll was vaporized. The "most severe effects of nuclear testing were felt around the world." Our government, for military secrecy, to allay public fears, for fear of possible legal action, and just plain lack of knowledge, tried to withhold information. "Some exposure related incidents have been revealed due to the impossibility of hiding them: namely the high radiation exposures of the Marshallese and the Japanese aboard the Fifth Lucky Dragon after the Castle Bravo disaster—information has slowly come to light in bits and pieces over the past 20 years.

Basic findings: Most important study, by National Cancer Institute in 1997. Internal exposure to radioiodine(1-131) was most serious health consequence, contaminating milk, effect especially strong in children. Millions of average Americans at the time received a thyroid radiation exposure of 2 rads, with some people receiving up to 300 rads. Roughly 120,000 extra cases of thyroid cancer (highly treatable, as cancers go) can be expected to develop, resulting in some 6,000 deaths. For comparison, the worst industrial disaster in history (Bhopal, India, 3 December 1984) killed about 300 people and injured 150,000." www.angelfire.com The Bhopal catastrophe was also a United States corporation "mistake".

The early tests were staged as grand performances with thousands watching. U.S. servicemen were instructed to lower their eyes and cover their heads with their arms. atomic veterans of America.com Only gradually did we begin to learn the planet-threatening dangers of what we were playing with. After 1962 all U.S. atomic tests have been underground. Along the way 11 nuclear bombs have been lost in accidents, never recovered.www.brook.edu

U.S. military personnel who were present at tests are still filing form NV-191 reporting exposure to harmful radiation. www.angelfire.com Our doctors, of course, wear lead protective vests, or leave the room, when they take our X-ray photos.

An article in The New York Times, July 6, 2004, tells the unbelievable story of nuclear waste from manufacture of first bombs, dropped on Hiroshima and Nagasaki—still without proper storage, after sixty years. The "temporary" storage in Ohio is described as "the basement from hell".

The Energy Department "wants to bury the materials at the Nevada Test Site", but Nevada says "no". They argue that the waste is radioactive that it would be a health hazard even to transport them and, even more, to bury them in unlined trenches.

CHAPTER 4

Incompetent Parenting

Our fourth terrible mistake is CHILD ABUSE. Beginning right at birth, we hurt our youngest most sensitive citizens in totally unnecessary ways, thinking we are "scientific" and "modern". Only moments after birth we put stinging medicine in their eyes ("to prevent venereal disease", when it could have been tested and prevented in other ways.) We cut off the natural protective skin from the most sensitive part of boy babies, through circumcision, a painful and unnecessary procedure aimed at cleanliness—which of course can be achieved without pain with every day soap and water. We abandoned natural breast feeding—feeding babies manufactured formula—won over by advertising to believe this was "modern" and "scientific."

We did gradually learn the many advantages of natural breast feeding: postponing pregnancy by providing a naturally broader spacing of babies (two years or more), preventing infant disease through natural hormones and anti-bodies passed on to the baby from the mother's immune system. It also allows the baby's jaws and teeth to develop more naturally, with less thumb-sucking. And of course there is nothing in the world to compare with the love and warm close tenderness of a nursing mother and baby.

But the food manufacturers never lose sight of the $$billions they can earn in profits. They have persuaded mothers all around the world to abandon breast feeding and buy the manufactured modern formulas. I know one father on a Caribbean island who couldn't even afford to buy a pair of pants because of the expensive baby formula, a totally unnecessary sacrifice, since the mother's milk was healthier—and free!

Even today in the United States there are thirty different baby formulas on the market. On the positive side, there are also organizations teaching young parents the many advantages of natural prepared childbirth and breast feeding. (See lamaze.org and lalecheleague.org) But I'm sure that U.S. baby formula manufacturers are hard at work in China advertising that manufactured baby formula is "modern, scientific, better for your baby." Just think of the profits U.S. companies could make if every baby in China drank formula!

Far too many families in the U.S. are examples of incompetent parenting, ranging from harsh abuse to dangerous permissiveness, from brutality to spoiling. In the early days of this country children did their share of family work, their "chores". They milked the cows, pumped and carried water, fed the chickens, cared for younger children, gathered firewood, herded livestock, helped cook, washed dishes, did their share of cleaning and laundry. They enjoyed a few homemade toys and games, learned skills—and felt important.

In contrast, today, even in the happiest families, children seldom have chores. Instead they are swamped with store-bought toys, spend hours sitting in front of television, all too often are exposed to verbal and physical fights between parents, do not have the chance to feel they are an important part of the family.

It is the rare family where children have regular chores, such as taking out trash and garbage, cleaning and dusting, washing dishes (even filling the dishwasher!), mowing the grass. Instead of learning to handle sharp knives and heavy hammers—safely—they are yelled at not to touch them. They are seldom taught how to have their own savings and checking account, earn money, and do their part in the family business. Too often they become "spoiled brats."

Someone has estimated from a poll that U.S.parents spend a bare 38 minutes a week in meaningful conversation with their kids. These children see 200,000 violent acts on television by age 18. TV statistics.

Tragically, the above occur in our happiest families. In our unhappiest, abuse and neglect led to 1,300 child fatalities in 2001, children 5 and younger the most frequent victims. One or both parents caused 83 percent of these deaths, other caretakers 17 percent.—US Department of Health & Human Services

CHAPTER 5

Growing Debts, No Savings

Even though some U.S. corporations are making $$billions around the world, millions of average Americans are rapidly getting into DEBT, misusing credit cards, buying unnecessary expensive luxuries with time payments and high interest, never learning to save. It's like a disease, passed on from parents to children. Very few are learning to automatically have part of their paycheck go into a savings account each week. Some try to fool themselves into thinking they can save a little at the end of the week, but few can do it that way. I can't. Our children can't. We are trying to learn to save by having the bank take a percentage automatically from our paycheck each week, before we ever see it. Maybe you can help us learn to save—so that we can buy more of the many wonderful products MADE IN CHINA.

Credit card debt is threatening a frightening number of American individuals and families. Few are able to pay their bills on time each month. The credit card companies purposely make it easy (to get in debt) by offering partial payments, offering cards to virtually anyone, regardless of credit rating. Students are targeted in a "predatory manor." Predatory means "out to make a killing."

If we try to save, economize, by buying a used car, we still have to pay sales tax. If a car is sold and resold four times, a sales tax must be paid—four times.

Our government doesn't help us to save. Even when we do save a little, at tax time they not only tax us on our earnings, but then a second time on the interest on our savings. Not fair! Easy credit and time payments make it hard to save, and easy to buy things we don't need. In the U.S., loans exceed savings by 700%. How can we save when we spend 10% more than we earn? Except for slight rises in 1998 and 2000, our saving went down annually from 1995 to 2001.

In the U.S. we have no good role model, for our government is also in debt "a little"—the number is so huge I had to check the dictionary to learn how to say it—over seven trillion—so large they write it differently in Britain. Soon we may have to create new words. On the U.S. National Debt Clock on the Web it says: $7,168,666,643,611.11 as of 12 April, 2004. There are about 293,799,370 of us, so apparently the share for each of us is $24,401.53. For the past six months this debt has been growing at an average of $1.98 billion—per day.

During the sad days of the Great Depression beginning in 1929 there was a saying: "Brother, can you spare a dime?" Will we be saying that again?

CHAPTER 6

$$ Billions For Pills

Some mistakes that millions of us in the United States are making are far more serious than money—we are getting SICK and DYING UNNECESSARILY—heart attacks, cancer, diabetes. We are spending more and more $$billions on medicines, doctors, hospitals—while death rates continue to rise—rather than simply following healthy natural inexpensive ways of living.

We haven't learned that prevention is far better than cure. The majority of Americans still feel that the only solution for illness is to go to a doctor, take medicines. A few are learning that it is faster, cheaper, and more effective—to study, REMOVE THE CAUSES, and seek healthier life styles. Probably one of our very greatest mistakes is that so many have not learned that they themselves, are the ones who can do the most to achieve good health.

Our women buy "Premarin", made with Estrogen from "PREgnant MARe's urINe", even though manufacturers have been warned for decades that it increases cancer risk up to 15 times, as Impotency, Infertility & Reproductive Disease Skyrocket. Men's prostate cancer is now #1, 200% higher than lung cancer!" Dr. Richard Schulze.

Our men have experienced a steadily falling sperm count. There are numerous theories as to the causes—Estrogen (in our water supplies which originated in birth control pills), salt, pesticides, radiation. Male fish are being "feminized" and other wildlife affected. www.ourstolenfuture.org We hope you will help us find the solutions.

Pick up the National Geographic, or any major magazine, and you will find numerous pages advertising medicines, almost always to treat "symptoms", seldom if ever to prevent or cure. A typical one is PLAVIX. Typically, one page in full color tries to sell. Then the following two pages in fine print (almost too small to read) give Adverse Reactions, Warnings, Precautions, Side Effects, Dangers of Overdose.

There are a minority like my wife and I, who study health constantly, work out daily at the health club, and do not take any doctor prescribed medications at all (except in case of surgery or hospitalization).

Polluted drinking water is a growing problem here, and worldwide. More and more of us are forced to buy distilled water, thought to be the healthiest solution. Even bottled "spring water" may have unknown contaminants.

The way our schools concentrate on team sports to produce winners, rather than FITNESS for everyone, does not result in lifelong health for all U.S. citizens. The typical U.S. school has a big budget for football, basketball, and baseball, while the majority of the students are neglected. We do not make every student a swimmer, as it was in Australia fifty years ago I was told (but have not been able to confirm if it is still true). Maybe someday this will be part of every school system worldwide. Sadly, even football stars are not destined for a long life of good health. Team sports are not suited for lifelong enjoyment and health. Much better are tennis and swimming.

In the 1950's Bonnie Prudden, pioneer fitness instructor and author, used the Kraus-Weber fitness tests on school children. The shocking result was to discover that U.S. children were way down in ability compared to others around the world. They rode in school buses, sat in front of television, did no physical exercise—and were in bad shape.

The publicity did have some good results. Bonnie Prudden helped motivate the founding of the President's Council for Physical Fitness, wrote many books, and is still spending her life promoting fitness, and training many others to do the same.

Of course getting fat, getting sick, and being in very sad physical condition are all closely interrelated. Maybe the saddest thing is that so few Americans are able to realize this and put it all together in a healthy life style, as outlined in Dr. Joel Fuhrman's new book, EAT TO LIVE—possibly the very best health book available.

CHAPTER 7

Wealth & Poverty

In a country where there is a great deal of freedom, but not the best universal education, too many decisions are made by the very WEALTHY for their own gain. The vast majority, through lack of knowledge, fail to vote and work for their own benefit. Nowhere is this more evident than in the giant mistakes in POWER GENERATION—over reliance on oil, coal, wood, atomic energy— very little research in solar, wind, geothermal, fuel cells. The power of big money invested in oil motivates the decisions of some presidents, even though environmentally harmful and potentially dangerous.

As this book nears publication a new documentary is making millions in theaters nationwide: "FAHRENHEIT 7/11". You might want to see it, a startling example of how free speech in America allows us to examine our own mistakes.

The problem of how to dispose of atomic wastes has no safe solution, since they remain dangerous for many thousands of years. Every politician votes against storage of wastes in his state, or even trucking it through, but continues to be in favor of atomic power— as long as it is not near his own home.

Wealth in government has steadily increased so that our representatives are too often motivated by self-gain rather than working for the benefit of those they represent. Our president receives almost half a million dollars, while even a congressman is paid $154,700 annually. usgovinfo

Our tax system benefits the wealthy—many millionaires, I've been told, paying no tax at all.

It is still the land of opportunity for those who have self confidence through early experiences of success, but we are not good at providing these experiences for everyone.

CHAPTER 8

Buying & Selling People

SLAVERY, unbelievably, was accepted as part of our economic culture, in the "land of the free". Church-going sea captains from New England (the northeastern corner of the U.S.) were among those who brought slaves from Africa to work on sugar cane plantations in the Caribbean islands and then the great cotton plantations of our southern states (as portrayed in the movie, "Gone With the Wind.")

This developed into what became known as the "triangular trade." (1st) U.S. ships brought slaves from Africa to the Caribbean to raise sugar cane, then (2nd) carried sugar (and rum made from sugar cane) to the U.S. to help subdue the Indians and pay hunters to kill the huge herds of wild buffalo, so that (3rd) the grasslands of the west could become available for us to raise cattle and become beef eaters, sending more shiploads of sugar and beef to England.

Slaves were bought and sold in the U.S. until the Civil War, but do not feel that the problems were all solved when the slaves were "free". Prejudice has continued and will continue on into the future. Great strides were made during the Civil Rights Movement, and continue. but our mistakes are not yet solved.

Other things we did might not be called outright slavery, but bordered on it.

We "explored" away a continent from the Indians, "imprisoning" them on tiny reservations. Over 500 tribes were exiled, often to barren land which our forefathers did not want. This led to poverty, up to 50% unemployment, illness, poor education, alcoholism, anger, and prejudice.

SID ANDERSON

No one knows how many native Americans were slaughtered by settlers and U.S. soldiers. One most terrible example is what happened in California during the 1848 gold rush. Of the estimated 150,000 Indians only about 31,000 survived in 1870. Many died from introduced diseases, but $5 was paid for each severed head in Shasta, 25 cents for each native American scalp in Honey Lake in 1863. The California state government in 1851 paid $1,000,000 reimbursement for scalping missions. About 4000 native American children were sold, young boys for up to $60, girls up to $200.

"In 1860 the Alta California reported a massacre conducted by a Captain Jarboe among the Achomawl peoples of the northeast. The attacking party rushed upon them, blowing out their brains, and splitting their heads open . . . little children in baskets, and even babes, had their heads smashed to pieces . . . one woman got into a pond hole, where she hid herself under the grass . . . her papoose on the bank in a basket. She was discovered and her head blown to pieces, the muzzle of the gun being placed against her skull, and the child was drowned in the pond." Google: Gold, Greed & Genocide

I strongly recommend you read ISHI IN TWO WORLDS, A Biography of the Last Wild Indian in North America by Theadora Kroeber (wife of the anthropologist who befriended him), University of California Press, Berkeley, CA 94720 1961. Also the video: Ishi, The Last Yahi, E9327.

In recent years, when tribal casinos bring in $$ billions—funding new homes, schools, and hospitals—doing more for tribal members than the U.S. government did in 300 years—everyone sees the benefits. Some are seeking new ways to improve casinos, to decrease the age-old dangers of gambling (debt, increased homicide rates, prostitution, homelessness) long associated with the worst of older casinos.

But most reservations are too isolated in the west to consider building casinos. An example is the Sioux Reservation, South Dakota, suffering from 18% unemployment, high birth rates and below average life expectancy, fourth highest child poverty rate. USDA PopulationReferenceBureau.

A powerful feature article with full page photo on cover was in PARADE, Sunday, May 16, 2004, nationwide: "Why We Must Return To Wounded Knee." To see photos and more information visit: www.parade.com, www.collegefund.com, www.sittingbull.edu

In World War II we put 107,000 of our own citizens in "prisons" which we called "Relocation Centers" or "Internment Camps"— for Americans of Japanese ancestry, forced by our government to leave their homes and farms. Some later distinguished themselves as soldiers. Few politicians today would care to try to justify our behavior, or even discuss it. www.trumanlibrary.org

Of course, the United States has always been unique among nations, a new home for millions who came voluntarily from all over the world, seeking freedom. We are "a melting pot". As our famous poet, Walt Whitman, said: "Here is not a nation, but a teeming nation of nations." AmericanImmigrationHomePage

Being a melting pot inevitably brought serious problems, very evident to this day. We have had many great leaders, such as Abraham Lincoln and Martin Luther King, as well as millions of virtually unknown citizens, who have spent their lives quietly working towards solutions.

But today, in 2004, though many across our land are not even aware, we still have slaves in the United States, young girls, bought and sold. See article in The New York Times, "The Girls Next Door", Jan. 25, 2004, and National Geographic, "21st Century Slaves", Sept. 2003, and others. Google: sex slavery in U.S., Moldova sex slaves.

We may not be the originators of this problem, but we allow it to continue. Girls in poor European countries such as Moldova are trapped by advertisements of "job as waitress in U.S.", but before they know what's happening they have been sold for $1000 and shipped off, never to have any freedom again. Like the drug mafia, their owners are ruthless, powerful, and unknown to the public. And like drug addicts there are millions of neurotic men out there, U.S. citizens, some in high places, who will not reveal the secret locations of these prison-brothels. These girls do not walk the streets, cannot leave their "prison", get no share of the income. They are slaves.

CHAPTER 9

Dreams of Winning

GAMBLING is an age-old addiction, like alcoholism, and drugs. Everyone recognizes its dangers, but in the United States state-run lotteries are used to raise money for government budgets, even for education, while the very people they claim to be helping are often suffering the most.

Gambling in the U.S. seems to be becoming more of a disease than a game. "Americans wager more than $400 billion a year, and that's just on legal gambling. The church and state used to rail against gambling; now the churches sponsor "bingo" and 36 states run lotteries. About 10 million Americans now have gambling-addiction problems, and cities with major gambling attractions report elevated crime rates, low-wage jobs and high-priced real estate." Public Concern Foundation Inc.

There are many ways to gamble—lotteries, casinos, and then—the stock market. It is considered a joke that the way to invest is to "buy high and sell low", but that is exactly what 80 million Americans did during 2001-2002. Our fantasies made us hang in there while even the "best" stocks went down and down—some to bankruptcy, often including massive internal fraud. The stock exchange has been called "the world's largest casino."

Statistically it is probable that you would have a higher chance of getting rich if you went crawling under the bushes in the park looking for lost money, rather than buying lottery tickets. But lottery tickets are sold at every gas station, and I have yet to see anyone crawling under the bushes.

CHAPTER 10

Gas Guzzlers

Unnecessary use of EXPENSIVE CARS, America's first love—not just economical transportation—it's an ego trip, an addiction! Many Americans love their car more than their wife or husband. When bored or up tight, they go for a drive. Out on the highway, with the wind in their hair, feeling the power of that engine, at least for the moment they are "King of the road!"

Cars, loss of public transportation, poor city and highway planning—are interrelated. From early teenage years, everyone wants a car. 17,448 were killed in alcohol related car crashes in 2001, 512,510 more were injured.-MADD MothersAgainstDrunkDriving

Airports, which could have been served by monorails, become traffic jams of private cars with giant expensive parking lots. Getting to and from the airport becomes an expensive and unpleasant part of a vacation. Air pollution is a serious health threat. Roadside trees die by the millions from exhaust fumes, browning trees very visible along busy roads. Auto time-payments at high interest keep millions in debt.

A few creative city planners have designed car-free inner communities where everyone can walk to school, stores, community center, swimming pool, ice rink, library, post office, ball fields, tennis courts. Hospitals, highways, and airports are reached by outer-circle roads and public transportation. But these communities have been too few, too late. Life could have been so much more pleasant and healthy.

Maybe you can be a city planner.

But it seems highway building never ends. To hop in the car to drive three blocks to buy cigarettes is not unusual.

CHAPTER 11

I Can't Go Home

No one knows how many UNPLANNED PREGNANCIES there are in the United States, because most of them are experienced by married couples, often the cause of a quick marriage in the first place, a marriage that too often might otherwise never have happened.

We do know, sadly, that approximately 22,000 U.S. children aged 14 or under get accidentally pregnant each year. Among teenagers 15 to 17 the numbers have been over 350,000, down to 290,00 in recent years, declining slightly each year for the past ten years. This decline is nothing to boast about however for the long range effects on these kids, their babies, and our entire society are saddening beyond our imagination. Obviously our education is not preparing our children to understand and safely plan their own lives. In contrast, Summerhill School in England, which does carefully educate their students, has never had a pregnancy in their 75 year history. summerhillschool.com

Instead of merely trying to prepare our students for a job, we need more creative teachers with the desire to prepare our children—for Life.

We often hear about "street children" around the world, "at least 100 million children worldwide believed to live at least part time on the streets." UNICEF, 29 March 1994. One might think that this is not a problem in the U.S.—far from it! "In the United States there is a crisis situation and Federal Government revealed that there are about 500,000 under-age runaways and "throw-aways. New York Times, 5 February 1990.

Yes, even here in the United States we have HOMELESS, STREET CHILDREN, with little or no schooling, sometimes working on the street or stealing, often having no home at all. The United Nations estimates there are 150 million children on the streets of big cities worldwide. Even in the U.S., the world's wealthiest nation, there are uncounted thousands, many victims of sex peddlers.

The Urban Institute has attempted to estimate the frightening numbers: "On any given night, over 37,000 people are homeless in New York City, including more than 16,000 children . . . The current number of shelter beds in the City was only 1,200 . . . Each night across America more than one million children have no place to call home . . . At least 2.3 million adults and children, or nearly 1 percent of the U.S. population."

The Ford Foundation estimates "nearly fifty percent of all homeless women and children are fleeing domestic violence" so, of course, all of our tragedies are inter-related.

In chapter 4 we talked briefly about incompetent parenting. Parents incapable of love, may abuse and force desperate children to leave home, joining the homeless on the streets, becoming victims of drug and sex peddlers. Covenant House, a chain of big city refuges, offers some of these street kids a chance to begin a new life. Many are often too terrified to explain why: "I can't go home."

In the U.S. and Europe some parents want to know in advance the sex of their unborn baby, or even choose and determine it. This is probably a sad mistake. If they truly want the joy of being parents to a child, they would be happy whatever its sex. Either a boy or a girl would be a wonderful surprise. But if they want to know in advance, maybe they need to spend more time thinking about their motives for parenthood.

It's interesting that more and more young couples are deciding to be non-parents, to enjoy other people's children.

CHAPTER 12

Chemicals In My Body

D RUG ADDICTION among youth, in city slums, and throughout our society is one of our saddest mistakes. We have allowed the world's largest market for addictive drugs to develop here in the United States. In the English language the word "drugs" is confusing because it has two meanings. First, it means medicines, manufactured by pharmaceutical companies to treat symptoms of chronic illness, prescribed by doctors, and sold in drug stores. But, secondly, it means addictive dangerous chemicals, manufactured illegally and secretly by criminals, transported internationally and sold illegally on the street by drug mafia and their hirelings.

Many people try to blame the problem on Colombia and other countries where cocaine, opium, heroin and other illegal addictive drugs are grown, manufactured and secretly shipped around the world. But they fail to face up to the fact that a large percentage is shipped to the U.S.—because the largest number of buyers and users are here. We have created the market, and allow it to exist.

CHAPTER 13

"Call Now !"

We are VICTIMS OF SALESMANSHIP, television commercials battering us for a large percentage of our viewing time. Except for our public radio and TV stations (which are supported by listener and viewer donations), our radio, TV, newspapers, and magazines are primarily funded by advertising: cars (to impress your friends), beauty aids (to "look younger"), heart burn and acid reflux medicines (to make up for poor eating habits), pain relievers and medicines (to recover from poor life styles), how to make a million quickly—each ending with the exclamation: "Call Now!"

Some of the most common commercials include hair restoration, weight loss programs and books, match-making to find your perfect lover, fast food, ways to stop smoking... The average American watches television over 3 hours a day, seeing 30,000 commercials a year—two million by age 65!

As you notice, many of our commercials are supposedly aimed at solving our major problems, but all too often are actually motivated by profit, and rarely actually solve problems.

CHAPTER 14

My Father Can't Read

Because of our inadequate school system, ILLITERACY, exists in these United States, leading to superstition, delinquency, and crime. "1 in 5 adults in the United States functions at the lowest literacy level. That means they lack the basic literacy skills they need to drive a car, use a computer, or get a decent job."—U.S. government sponsored National Adult Literacy Survey, 1993.

Too many children are forced to admit, "My father can't read." In 2002 2,902,000 adults (not in institutions) had less than a fourth grade education. US Census

The National Institute for Literacy says that a shocking "23 million Americans are functionally illiterate", nearly all in our largest cities.

"39% of Boston seniors could not name the 6 New England states. 63% of Minneapolis seniors could not name all seven continents. 25% of Dallas seniors could not identify the country that borders the U.S. on the south." IlliteracyFacts.

Because so few Americans learn that we are part of a Universe operating on dependable laws, too many of us believe in ghosts, haunted houses, and other superstitions—or imagine they can control the roll of dice or the spin of a roulette wheel. Our wealthy seldom learn foreign languages when they travel, so become known as the "Ugly American."

It's exciting to see children in bilingual families easily learning two or more languages at once, in infancy, without being taught. Someday creative teachers will learn how to set the stage allowing this to happen for all children, instead of suffering in language classes later with little success. Google: children learn several languages easily.

CHAPTER 15

Gone With the Passenger Pigeons

The United States began on the eastern edge of a vast continent, environmentally almost untouched by the stone age cultures living here for thousands of years. But our early settlers brought steel tools, horses and cattle, sheep and pigs, wagons with wheels. The forests fell—as settlers moved westward, turning the virgin forests into farms, the grasslands into feed lots. The wonderful topsoil, thousands of years in the making, washed away down the streams and rivers, into the Mississippi to be lost in the Gulf of Mexico. A powerful documentary movie, "THE RIVER", made by the Tennessee Valley Administration (TVA), tells the story, beautifully and tragically, a chapter of U.S. history which should be seen by everyone. Much of it is from the early days of photography, frightening log jams being dynamited, ancient steamboats on the Mississippi River, poverty-stricken farm families forced to move west. THE RIVER A03630VNB1 is available for $60 from NTIS, 5285 Port Royal Rd., Springfield, VA 22161, www.ntis.gov 800-553-NTIS. This movie also raises questions about building giant dams.

And so began the sad years of ENVIRONMENTAL DEGRADATION, leading to unregulated hunting and the beginning of ENDANGERED SPECIES. Passenger Pigeons, once brightening the skies in seemingly endless flocks, were slaughtered wholesale by Americans, becoming extinct in 1914.

POLLUTION, even with federal and state regulation, is doing life-threatening harm to our air, drinking water, soil, rivers, lakes, oceans. A large percentage of citizens, as is true around the world, now buy their water. Coming out from an air conditioned restaurant onto a hot summer sidewalk, too many Americans discover that their hometown—stinks!

Recycling, emissions controls on factory smoke stacks, environmentally friendly new methods of treating sewage and garbage are making slow progress. Sadly, most corporations are fighting environmental progress, rather than using their expertise to make protecting the environment profitable.

Our factories were historically located on rivers or seacoasts, considered to be unpollutable. But today fish in the world's furthest oceans contain health-threatening industrial chemicals.

Most factories need clean water in their manufacturing process. Some humorists suggest that laws be passed requiring all factories to have their water intake pipe downstream from their waste discharge.

One leading world manufacturer of chocolate products, NESTLE, has a factory on the river in our hometown. Their effluent pipe had such a foul smell that boaters learned to pass on the far side of the river—except for one friend wishing he could put a bottle of it behind the boss's desk—who would order his employees to "get rid of that stench immediately!"

"Faced with the threat of being completely submerged if sea levels continue to rise, worried officials from almost 40 small island states gathered in Majuro, Marshall Islands, this week to hammer out a united position on lowering global emissions of greenhouse gases . . . sea level projected to rise 37 inches by 2100. Two small islands of the Pacific nation of Kiribati have already disappeared . . . small island nations contribute only 0.6 percent of global greenhouse gas emissions. It is fitting that the talks are being held in the Marshalls, where the highest point is less than seven feet above sea level." Environmental News Network

"The leaders of Tuvaly—a tiny island country in the Pacific Ocean midway between Hawaii and Australia—have conceded defeat in their battle with the rising sea, announcing that they will abandon their homeland (the first, but certainly not the last.) . . . not a new issue . . . in 1987, President of Maldive islands, gave an impassioned address at United Nations . . . his country of 311,000 an endangered nation, most of its 1196 tiny islands barely 2 meters above sea level.

In 2000 the World Bank published a map showing that a 1-meter rise in sea level would inundate half of Bangladesh's rice land . . . forcing millions to migrate . . . already one of the most densely populated countries of the world.

In the U.S. beach front properties, much like nuclear power plants, are becoming uninsurable." EarthPolicyInstitute2000

The nations of the world have little sympathy with the U.S., since we produce the largest percentage of greenhouse gases, yet will not abide by the Kyoto Protocol. Worldwide details can be found by following Google to "rising sea levels".

The U.S. is still a leading cause of deforestation, mainly by being a market for the rest of the world. Even though Americans may not be wielding the chain saws, we are still highly responsible for the "70 acres per minute" of the world's forests being lost. rainforestalliance.org

There is no need for me to elaborate on how dangerously we are over-harvesting the resources and life of our Blue Planet.

A few wonderful organizations are learning how to help people around the world use natural resources "sustainably", assuring that they can continue to do business profitably—forever. Check out: rainforestalliance.org

CHAPTER 16

Hopalong Cassidy

As the westward expanding United States explored away a continent from the Indians, not caring that it had been their homelands for thousands of years, gun-toting heroes and villains were made "famous" by legends and Hollywood movies. Childhood toys and games made us believe that problems could—and should—be solved with guns. HAND GUNS became a part of American history and culture, and probably are more widely used today than ever.

The "right to bear arms" has been deep in our tradition, but there is ongoing controversy about how easy it should be to buy a hand gun. There is no federal requirement that handguns be registered, though 44% to 80% of Americans feel they should be. Of course gun manufacturers fight this trend. americansforgunsafetyfoundation

"One American young person is killed by gunfire every hour, making firearms the second leading killer of youths, after accidents. Change isn't easy when members of Congress pocket millions in campaign contributions from the National Rifle Association." Public Concern Foundation Inc.

More statistics: Of "estimated 192 million firearms in civilian hands, 65 million are handguns. In 1997 there were 89 deaths per day, or a firearm death every 16 minutes. For every firearm death, there are nearly three gun injuries requiring emergency medical treatment, costing about $4 billion a year in medical expenses. Every federal Court of Appeals that has considered the meaning of the Second Amendment (the right to bear arms) has held that it protects the right of states to maintain a militia, not an individual right to own a gun." Violence Policy Center, Guns in America, Police Foundation, 1996.

I would like to end this chapter with a humorous story, which gives another view of how deeply seated handguns are in our culture. My uncle, in the State Department, told this story as though it were true:

"At a State Department dinner I found myself seated beside the charming young wife of a foreign diplomat. She turned to me asking: 'Mr. Sullivan, could you help me get a chastity belt?' My face must have turned a deep red, as I stuttered: 'A chastity belt?' (In the Middle Ages, chastity belts reportedly were locked onto wives by jealous husbands to prevent unfaithfulness.) She replied, turning close to me with a charming smile: 'Yes, I want it for my son." More embarrassed than ever, I barely managed to say: 'For your son?' She smiled again, 'Yes, I hear that all the boys in your country have them, a Hopalong chastity belt.' (Hopalong Cassidy was a movie hero who wore the traditional gun belt, with two holsters for fast-draw six-shooter pistols, sold everywhere in the United States in toy stores as a Hopalong Cassidy belt, on the web from Sagebrush Entertainment, Inc.)

CHAPTER 17

Chernobyl Couldn't Happen Here

In POWER GENERATION we are behind the times. The U.S. is still removing fossil fuels from the ground (coal, oil, gas), and mining uranium for atomic power plants, even when far better and environmentally safer technology is already available, such as wind turbines, solar panels, and hydrogen fuel cells.

Our President Bush did recently allot money to promote fuel cells, but his concern for the environment could only be described as very low. He is inexperienced, and not aware of the implications for his children and grand children, and the future of mankind.

The story has been going around that the Bush library recently burned to the ground. However, it wasn't too serious because there were only three books in it, and two of them he hadn't finished coloring yet. hahaha.com (origin unknown)

Many feel we made a big mistake in electing a president who is inexperienced, and feels war is a good way to try to solve problems. My wife, born in Scotland, still has a British passport. She says she will become a U.S. citizen when there's a candidate she would like to vote for, but it hasn't happened yet.

One day at New York's JFK Airport, waiting for our limo to Connecticut, my wife and I were curious about the twenty or so very young children sitting in a row on the floor, against the wall opposite us. It was Dec. 3, 1991. I know, because in our home is a very beautiful lacquer bowl with a note of that date taped to it—which still brings a tear to our eyes.

Sports teams, or groups of teenagers on trips, are common in airports, but children aged seven or eight seemed unusual. They were very quiet, no laughing or playing. Two young women with them also were quiet and serious.

Were they Russian? Where could they be going? Finally, I walked over to speak with the women. They were indeed Russian, from near Chernobyl, suffering from radiation sickness from the atomic power plant disaster of April 16, 1986, on their way to a health camp in Oregon. "We have four hours to wait, no money for food. It's a long hard trip for these children."

I walked back to tell the sad news to my wife. As always, the children of the world suffer the most from mistakes of adults.

After the meltdown at Chernobyl, radiation drifted downwind across many countries, from Ukraine and Belarus into Lithuania, Latvia, Estonia, on into Finland, Sweden, Norway, and around the world. Herds of reindeer used for milk in Lapland had to be destroyed. Especially where it rained, mushrooms, potatoes, and other crops could not be eaten.

We remembered we had a $100 bill left over from our vacation in Puerto Escondido. It could easily have been spent in Mexico, and soon would be gone—for who knows what. We walked back over, telling the women that sadly it wouldn't go far at airport prices. We wished we could sit down and talk with the kids, but the only Russian word we knew was "niet", a sad commentary on those "cold war" years! One of the women came over with the beautiful lacquer bowl. Our limo came, and we were off to Connecticut. We were the richer, and have been ever since.

That was over twelve years ago. When our granddaughters heard the story, they wanted to know how the children were. They might be out of high school by now—we hoped. We were forced to admit that their stories may not all have happy endings. Radiation causes thyroid disease and cancer.

Chernobyl was a major world catastrophe, and might have been infinitely worse. Overconfident workers broke at least six safety rules. Water reaching the red hot 1700-ton graphite core started over twenty fires, detonating gas "hurling radioactive debris a mile into the sky, probably coming close to an atomic explosion." The world knew nothing until on April 28 Sweden measured radiation 14 times higher than normal.

Soviet efforts to contain the radiation were dangerously heroic. Helicopters dropped 5000 tons of lead, boron, and other materials on the exposed core. 31 firemen and plant workers died. By November a giant "sarcophagus" of steel and 410,00 cubic meters of concrete was hastily built over the plant. 135,000 people were evacuated, cattle and sheep slaughtered, the town and surroundings becoming a no-man's-land. Soviet estimates said half the fallout dropped within 35 kilometers, but the other half fell on more than twenty countries worldwide. In Italy and other countries officials advised people not to drink milk. Two years later wild mushrooms in Germany were so radioactive that to eat them would be "playing Russian radiation roulette." A scientist at the University of California, Dr. Goldman, conservatively estimated that worldwide deaths from Chernobyl-induced cancers would be over 40,000 (12,000 Soviet, 21,000 European, 7,000 around the world.) NUCLEAR AGE

I phoned the State of Oregon Health Department, but was never able to learn more about these children. We can only wonder and hope for their future.

There is great difference of opinion, but many wonder if now might be the time to begin phasing out all atomic power plants—for the children of the future.

Children who lived downwind from Chernobyl are still developing thyroid disease and thyroid cancer, families evacuated, lives disrupted, food and firewood still contaminated. United Nations report. The Ukrainian National Chornobyl Disaster Museum in Kiyev, has website: ic-chernobyl.kiev

Some sources give more frightening estimates: "in addition to other approximately 30 people killed instantly, more than 15,000 died in the emergency clean up afterwards. Experts reckon that radiation equivalent to 500 times that released by the atom bomb dropped on Hiroshima was measured in the atmosphere around

Chernobyl . . . altogether around 3.5 million people, over a third of them children, are believed to have suffered illnesses as a result of radioactive contamination. U.N. figures show that millions in Ukraine, Belarus and Russia still live on contaminated land." www.coldwar.org www.chernobyl.info

Those who feel it could never happen in the U.S. seem to forget about 3-Mile Island, where it almost did, and a dozen other "minor" accidents. Some try to feel Chernobyl was not a major catastrophe, even though radiation spread around the world. Maybe we should all see "Chernobyl Heart", the 2004 Oscar-winning short documentary.

Disposal or storage of nuclear waste is still unsolved. Nevada's Yucca Mountain will not be ready till 2010 at the earliest. Some have even recommended rocketing waste to the sun. Sadly, 5% of rockets launched internationally—explode. It would take about 31 rockets to carry currently stored waste, a risk few would consider. Popular Science, Dec. 2003, Nagging Questions.

CHAPTER 18

Civilize 'em With a Cragg

The United States. has too often been a self-appointed "GLOBAL POLICEMAN." Enough said.

For those who would like details, see A CENTURY OF U.S. MILITARY INTERVENTIONS, www.swans.com/library/art6/zig055.html These range from the massacre of 300 Lakota Indians at Wounded Knee in 1890—through Argentina, Chile, Hawaii, Nicaragua, China, Korea, Panama, Philippines, Cuba, Puerto Rico, Guam, Samoa, Honduras, Dominican Republic, Mexico, Russia, Yugoslavia, Guatemala, Turkey, El Salvador, Iran, Uruguay, Greece, Vietnam, Lebanon, Laos, Indonesia, Oman, Angola, Libya, Grenada, Bolivia, Virgin Islands, Saudi Arabia, Somalia, Bosnia, Haiti, Croatia, Zaire, Liberia, Albania, Sudan. Afghanistan, Yugoslavia, Iraq . . .

I remember snatches of a song I heard as a boy in Shanghai, supposedly sung by U.S. 4th Marines sent to prevent uprisings in the Philippines:

> "Damn, damn, damn the Philippinoes!
> Pockmarked yellow skinned ladrones (robber-bandits)
> Civilize 'em with a Cragg (rifle)
>   . . . and then
> Go sailing back to our beloved home."

It is tragic, in so many ways, that soldiers, totally unprepared to do anything constructive in another culture, too often increase prejudice on both sides. Local citizens are obviously unhappy about their presence. The real problems, plus many new ones, are seldom solved until long after the soldiers have left. Once again, cultural exchange during many previous years, might have made sending soldiers unnecessary.

CHAPTER 19

Exponential Growth

Possibly our greatest mistake of all involves our future, our children's future, the future of mankind. The United States is neglecting our responsibility in the Family of Man, by not doing our part to help slow the WORLD POPULATION EXPLOSION. Poverty and disease in any part of the world affects us all. Failure here could ensure failure in all our other problems.

Turning your computer to the World POP Clock (U.S. Census Bureau), it's very sobering to watch the numbers grow (too rapidly to count verbally) as 5 babies are born each second around the world, with ever-increasing momentum—far out of balance with the two deaths each second.

"There are 1.2 billion people, nearly 20 percent of the 6.3 billion living today, between the ages of 10 and 19, the largest adolescent generation ever; their reproductive decisions could ultimately determine whether the earth's human numbers will level off at 8 billion or less, or at 10 billion or more. How they handle the awesome responsibility of parenting . . . will mean the difference between us having a good quality of life, or all of us heading for an environmental Armageddon.

Africa is the fastest growing region in the world, with a current population of 861 million projected to reach nearly 1.29 billion by 2025 and approach 1.9 billion by 2050, a 120 percent increase in only 50 years." Fifty million children in sub-Saharah Africa have no schooling. Population Institute 2003

These children, tragically, are probably less prepared for achieving a happy life than any generation of children the world has ever known.

Many feel that this unplanned population explosion is at the root of all other problems. Population is not growing at a steady rate. It is growing—exponentially—at a faster and faster momentum.

The US government has cut down on support of worldwide family planning. We are not talking about abortion, which virtually no one wants. It is sometimes the desperate last resort for people who do not have birth control knowledge or access, or the ability to plan the spacing and number of their children. It is not infrequent for women to come for help—bleeding—after using a coathanger wire or other crude implement in desperation. Statistics show overwhelmingly however that when birth control is available, the number of abortions drops dramatically, and families are smaller and happier.

Our current politicians have cut down on support of international family planning, seemingly unaware that smaller and happier families around the world will benefit everyone, including our own children in the United States. They fear losing the votes of religious groups who mistakenly feel that family planning promotes abortion. Some think they will have a more prosperous future if there is an increasing number of customers, but this may not be true if these potential "customers" are too poor to buy.

On March 10, 2004, in Santiago, Chile, of 41 nations present, only the U.S. delegation voted "NO" to participate in world commitment "to tackle the problem of rapid population growth in the developing world, including its impact on the environment. Over the last 30 years, as world population has climbed 60 percent, U.S. support for international family planning has declined by 40 percent." UNFPA World Population Report

But, you say, in many parts of the world population growth has stopped, is even decreasing. Yes, in Japan and some countries of Europe this is true. The growing number of elderly often have no one to help support them. But it is probable that in these wealthy countries solutions will be worked out.

Sadly, the future happiness for all the world's children, including our own, is being played out in Africa, northern India, Asia, and South America. In Kenya, Malawi, and Zambia 15% have HIV/AIDS, bringing the rate of population growth almost to a stop—but in the process there are uncounted children living in shanty town shacks built from scraps, sometimes ten to a room—often all of these children are orphans.

In most of the other African countries the rate of population growth is terrifying. By 2050 population is expected to grow by 230% in Angola, 255% in Mayotte, 286% in Madagascar, 330% in Niger, compared to 45% in the United States, 1% in Austria,— 21% in Japan. Population Reference Bureau www.prb.org Is this really any concern of ours? Will it affect our children and grandchildren? You might want to get the 2004 NOVA video, "World in the Balance", and make up your own mind.

On the positive side, we do have one of the most effective private organizations in the world working for international family happiness, Population Communications International. They believe that from the dawn of history "story telling" has been a primary force in education and motivation in every culture, from shamans around the campfire to modern day radio and television "soap operas". PCI carefully adapts stories to each culture, with highly successful programs in China (Bai Xing, "ordinary people", on CCTV, has won six awards), Mexico, Caribbean, South America, Africa, India, Pakistan, with many new programs developing each year. Send for their fascinating free literature: PCI, 777 United Nations Plaza, NY, NY 10017 Phone toll free 877-PCI-SOAP, or visit their newly redesigned website: population.org

The following graph shows the frightening reality of exponential growth:

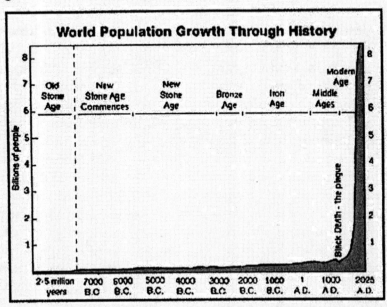

Sources: Population Ref. Bureau & UN World Population Projections to 2100

As you see, for thousands of years population grew quite slowly, at an even rate. Then the rate started increasing—not just the total numbers but the RATE of increase. This rate of increase continued to speed up. "About 1650, we WENT AROUND THE BEND of the J-curve as our numbers started growing EXPONENTIALLY. Nothing in the world can sustain exponential growth." Audubon

Another way to understand the overwhelming power of exponential growth in population is to measure the DOUBLING TIME.

It took from the dawn of history to 1804 for us to reach 1 billion—over 2000 years We then surged, by 1927 reaching 2 billion—only 123 years

Our rate of growth increased so that by 1974 we had reached 4 billion—a mere 13 years

Passing 6 billion in 1999, even with HIV-AIDS, we are now projected to double—one more time—by 2028, taking us to: 8 billion—in 54 years . . . www.overpopulation.org

"There has been more growth in population since 1950 than during the 4 million years since our ancestors first stood upright." Richard Estrads

"If fertility remained at current levels, the population would reach the absurd figure of 296 billion in just 150 years." A Special Moment in History, McKibben, May '98, Atlantic Monthly

Of course, the present rates of growth will NOT continue forever. They cannot. Our Earth is too small. Catastrophe would build on catastrophe. Like lemmings, we would run out of land, our world's water supplies becoming fatally polluted, food sources disappearing, cities outgrowing their ability to handle sewage and crime, disease swamping our health facilities, governments giving way to anarchy—how would it end?—We don't know—It might be atomic war. It might be devastating world wide plagues beyond imagining. It might be such an overwhelming increase in global warming, that world agriculture would be devastated by changing climate and storms of unheard of intensity. It might be a combination of all of these.

* * *

Luckily we don't need to wait passively to find out.

There are thousands of exciting things we can do to help prevent these tragedies from happening, to assure a happier life for our children and grandchildren.

SUNSET, SUNRISE

We will not try to list all of the mistake of the U.S. That would require more than one book. I'm sure you have been filling in many which I neglected to mention.

When we look at human beings, it is overwhelming to see the extremes of our ERRORS and at the same time the WONDERS of our capabilities—music, art, science, sports, health, happiness. It is truly awesome to imagine what the world—could be.

So sometimes, at sunset, or sunrise, we pause—to wonder. Where have we gone astray? Why have we gone astray? Could all the world's children be enjoying the best that we human beings are capable of?

Some feel that this is impossible. We just have to look out for ourselves, let the others sink or swim.

Many others feel that this great Blue Planet is now One World. We are the Family of Man.

What affects the happiness of anyone in the world is important for us also. What is best for everyone in the world will turn out to be best for ourselves.

When I was a boy on Lushan I had a very favorite place where I used to go, by myself—a rocky ridge above "the Thousand Steps", where the mountain drops away with frightening steepness to the distant rice fields. It was almost silent, distances too great to hear a bus or river boat 4000 feet below. Only the breeze, in the grass, and on my cheek—an occasional bird.

Almost like a soaring eagle, my view took in hundreds of miles of the mighty Yangtze River, flowing from the sunset clouds billowing in the west to the misty distant east—leading in my imagination to Nanjing, Shanghai, and all of China, my Great Teacher, stretching "forever" past the horizons.

I would sit there quietly, alone, dreaming of the future.

And now, you have joined me.

We sit there together, on the rocks, at sunset, dreaming of sunrises to come . . . our future . . . the future of China . . . the United States . . . the World . . .

END

$$$$ Part-time jobs available $$$$
Promote this book
Write for FREE details
Grand Opportunity, Box 187, Hawleyville, CT 06440 USA

For publication rights in China
Contact the author in care of the publisher, Xlibris.com

For motion picture rights
Contact the author in care of the publisher, Xlibris.com

Once upon a time . . . in China
there was an American boarding school
on top of a sacred mountain
400 miles up the Yangtze River!

Unparalleled opportunities at this moment in history
for use of documentaries, and on-location filming:
  Coolies towing boats in Yangtze gorges
  Climbing LuShan in ice storm
  US students vaccinating farmers for smallpox
  Sinking of USS Panay, river gunboat on Yangtze
  Hong Kong, boat people, floating restaurant
  Shanghai sidewalk opium dens
  US Marines racing rickshaws
  US students climbing into train steam engine
  Exploring battle fields, US student losing finger
  Truck riding in Shanghai
  Shanghai American School graduation
  Girl with red rose on Shanghai Bund

My very special thanks to:

Ai-Ping Zhu, Connecticut
Pinjie Ren, Harvard student
Moon dehua, President, Chamber of Commerce, LuShan
—most of all, to China, My Great Teacher